Journey in the Mind's Eye of a Poet: A Search for Faith

BOOK THREE (2008 TO 2009)

The Book of Lost and Found
or Chasing Rainbows

Tony Prewit

Journey in the Mind's Eye of a Poet: A Search for Faith
Book Three (2008 to 2009): The Book of Lost and Found
or *Chasing Rainbows*

copyright Tony Prewit, 2012, all rights reserved

Published by Ridgeline Press
Silver City, New Mexico, U.S.A.
ISBN 978-0-9854487-2-1

Editing, book design, cover design, and production services by
Heidi Connolly, Harvard Girl Word Services
Cover artwork by Tony Prewit

Acknowledgments

I would like to thank my wife, Patricia Prewit, for the years of assistance in sorting, editing, and proofreading all my work. I thank her most of all for her being her and allowing me to continue to be the person she married. I would also like to thank Sarah Johnson, a professional proofreader, who offered intelligent suggestions in shaping these books and gave me a valuable critique of its quality and content. Finally, I would like to thank the friends who read the complete series, contributed valuable suggestions, and urged me to arrange it into the form it has become: Gretchen Van Auken, Charlie Mckee, and Gail Rein. I thank Raymond Hornbaker for the years of commitment to our late-night discussions. I would also like to mention the editor who helped with the final sculpture of these books, Heidi Connolly, whose vision, talent, and professional guidance have been invaluable.

Table of Contents

Prologue

These six books are written in a poetry/prose form, a process that spans thirty-five years and encompasses the gradual evolution into my inner search for a personal faith and belief in God. It is a poet's journal and also like a novel in poetry form, one in which I am the narrator as well as a main character. The poems document my gradual disengagement with traditional, conservative, evangelical Christianity as I built a belief and faith of my own. Although I certainly did not have this defined purpose when I started this journal, it matured this way over time to become collection of six books that record a journey in search of a faith I could call my own.

As I walk away from the Christianity in which I once believed without doubting the existence of a God, I continue to discover a place within where I am learning how to build my own faith. This writing is for those who are at a dead end or a crossroad in their belief, or in a dysfunctional relationship (so to speak) with their spiritual beliefs. One of my messages, therefore, is that our spiritual beliefs do not have to be unchangeable.

Consequently, these poems are not so much a criticism of Christianity as they are a process of learning to ask the right questions. Over time I have learned to be wary of those who do not want to hear my questions and who are defensive toward honest doubt and inquiry. Because I was trapped in a doctrine that did not allow me to express my belief in my own way, and because I wanted to keep my Christian friends, I kept silent for many years.

The poems in this work capture my observations and reflections about how I see life through the veil of my own struggle, and will hopefully allow others to consider the shortcomings of their own beliefs, or of any belief that does not allow for true dialog. Because none of us really knows the truth for sure when it comes to belief, it would appear that there are shortcomings in all spiritual belief systems, regardless of form. For that reason, we are left to ourselves to construct a satisfactory — and satisfying — faith.

The stunning effect of this pursuit is my finding that God gets larger from the inside out. This is where my journey has found its pleasure and its peace, even while admitting the sorrow and fear of the search.

I have wrestled with my soul along this path and it wrestled back, for what I was struggling with was my spiritual identity. In wrestling, I learned the value of putting forth the right questions rather than assuming I had the right answers.

In fact, questions have become answers in their own right for me, for a light turned on in the asking that helped illuminate my way. I further learned that without questions we have no way to really appreciate where we are going and why. As such, I am thankful that I realized the importance of questions within the arena of spiritual beliefs.

The six books in this series are (in order): *Journal of Time, Portals and Passages, The Book of the Lost and Found* or *Chasing Rainbows, Moods of War, The Source,* and *Another Day.*

Book one is the beginning of my realizations and observations of life, which I describe as "me looking inside me from the perspective of the outside me," and then, "me looking outside me from the perspective of the inside me." It is the discovery of my need for a faith in God of my own. Book two is a confession of my dreams and the effect dreams can have upon one's life. Book two also reveals my earliest thoughts concerning my spiritual beliefs (kept very secret until then). These secrets became a burden to my search for faith. In books three and four I begin to focus my writing toward a more intense spiritual inquiry and on my discontentment with religious answers. These two works became like a great mountain I needed to climb, blocking the path of what I considered my "true" journey. One might also describe them as an inner wrestling match where the rule was to fight to the finish. These books are the recording of how I lost my past faith and discovered what I call "conflicts of faith." Hence, book five is the result of feeling as if I had reached the top of the mountain, had a good view of a long way down the road, and could tell that although the journey was long from over, I was already sensing a peace that came from finding my own faith. Book six is about learning to live with the faith I had created.

Phrases and Words

The phrase "Treat others as we want them to treat us" is the most frequently used phrase in these books, and it has become more important to me as the years have passed. It has become a part of the foundation of my own faith because no matter how I might try, it stuck with me, withstanding all inquiry, doubt, and question.

To treat others as we want them to treat us simply means to me that we value others as equal to ourselves and value their needs as important as our own. And that if we do not wish to be cheated, lied to, deceived, oppressed, or manipulated, then we should be willing not to cheat, lie, deceive, oppress, or manipulate others.

I use other Judeo-Christian terms such as "heaven" and "hell" and the duality of "good" and "evil." These terms and their meanings come from my own culture and western traditional Christian teaching. I do not necessarily consider these terms to be universally accepted as truth; they serve only as my own points of reference into my inner spiritual search.

My use of the word "God" in the masculine form is habit and based somewhat on the limitations of the English language. In my mind, God is of no gender, no religion, no race, no culture.

In some parts you may find the writing in these books somewhat redundant. The repetitiveness serves as an accurate picture of my perspective, however, for I believe we are all in the process of being formed and we repeat our thoughts and feelings until they either become a part of us or fade.

My style of writing is varied. It weaves poetry, commentary, and prose. I do not attempt to stay inside the lines of strict grammatical compliance. I give myself poetic license. I am much more concerned with content and the work's original form than with adherence to rules. You'll see I have also invented a few words along the way.

Initially, my poetry/journal was not produced as a neat stack of notebooks; instead, scattered notebooks, legal pads, single sheets, and scratch paper filled with writings piled up until the notebooks piled up on top of each other. They were in no real order. No, I did not have a neat stack at all. In fact, after thirty-five years' worth of notebooks had turned into a kind of organizational nightmare, I felt it was almost futile to even attempt to sort through it all. Common sense prevailed, however, and this six-book format is the result of sorting and compiling a presentable record of my writings.

Part One:
Beginnings

The Journey to the Rainbow

spiritual journeys
trial and error
ongoing inquiry

> *mysterious God*
> *why so quiet?*
> *is silence your answer*
> *to our questions unanswered?*

many books
say they have
found You
yet my own soul
sees only seekers
chasing rainbows

> *are all images of God*
> *our own desire?*
> *are our fights with one another*
> *the real answers to our faith in God?*

i am writing
my own inquiry
for i have found
all others lacking

it may be
i am only searching
for an image of God
that will satisfy me

am i falling into
the book of the lost and found
chasing a rainbow
for a God i hope
waits for me at the end?

i cannot chase another's rainbow any longer
i must chase my own.

The Wall

1.

Walking rather briskly
feeling as if all was well
I came to a wall in the middle of my path
that prevented me from continuing

What was i to do? What was this wall anyway?
As I examined it I felt as if I were examining
a part of me that had to be climbed
or torn down or walked around

Whatever the decision, though
I knew I had to come to terms with this wall

I sat down and leaned back against it
and as I contemplated an intuitive knowing came to me
I realized what this wall represented
but did not know how to proceed

Should I turn around or climb it, go around it, or tear it down?

I knew now that this wall represented all the
failed theologies and truths of life
I have lived because I dared not challenge
or question them
And that now this wall had halted my journey
on the path of life

What was I to do about this wall?
Though uncertain, I knew that my discovery
of its presence was important
and that I must do something

Should I turn around or climb it, go around it, or tear it down?

    Convinced that I could not continue
    until I dealt with this wall
    I concluded that since it was my own dilemma
    how I came to terms with it
    would be my own choice

After much debate
I decided to tear the wall down
for it seemed a more permanent solution
than climbing over such a high obstacle
or walking around it
and I knew I would not turn back

This wall was somehow of my own making
How I dealt with it would be my own as well

A small shed by the wall beckoned — in it chisels, hammers, and shovels

The shed was also a part of my soul
and the tools inside were of patience, inquiry,
discernment, courage, compassion,
honesty . . . and others I did not recognize

I knew they were there for me to use
to assist me in tearing down my wall
but at first they were so burdensome
that I thought perhaps
it was better not to set about my task at all

I paused
I panicked
but soon began again

picking up each tool one at a time
and learning how to hold and work them
For it turned out that my fear of not trying
was greater than my fear of failure
and it was with relief that I learned
I could learn to handle these tools

So then I examined the wall and began
the work of bringing it down
And as all humans do
I soon learned the frustration of trial and error.

    2.

I started to chisel at the top of the wall
but soon found that chiseling at the zenith
and working my way down would not work
for the mortar and the brick were stubborn
and well placed

I rested awhile
and as I thought about my problem dozed off
When I woke suddenly
the fear of failure had grabbed me anew

Then out of nowhere an idea emerged
— perhaps digging at the foundation
where the earth was softer would be more suitable
than chiseling at the bricks

I surmised that after digging the wall would topple
As if time hurried me on I rarely looked up
Soon I had razed the wall's foundation
of failed theologies and truths

Upon examination of the wall I saw
that the mortar was nothing more than my own faith
that had held the bricks together so well

After the bricks fell
I saw that the wall's foundation
was composed of the fear to question these truths
as if questioning were a taboo that one did not
dare challenge

Suddenly I was seized by panic
What if the wall were for my own protection
placed here by God to keep me from crossing over?

Had I destroyed my own safety with God?
Was this fear placed in me by God?
Had I destroyed the safety that God had given me?

Was this the wall of God?
By destroying it would I destroy my relationship with Him?

The panic in me gradually dissolved
as I realized that this kind of fear-based belief
was not of the sort formed by the God
I believed in

The God of this wall
relies on teaching and proselytizing a belief
that states that *not believing* a certain way means
      – off to hell you go
And to *believe* their way means
      – off to heaven you go

Though fear plucked at me hard
it did not bear witness to the God in my heart

So I began to dig through the rubble of the
fallen wall to further examine its content
and gradually the fear of losing the wall faded

What had I gained from toppling this wall?
Was there something better on this path beyond the wall?

A nagging inside me said *there is something better*
and your peace was not here in this wall
You must continue your journey

I rose and began to walk away from the fallen wall
cautiously persevering on my journey
for this was not the wall of God
but only a wall that had become as a God to me
— *a wall of fear of my own making.*

Fear

Has God condemned us to Hell for merely
not becoming Christians?

To believe that Jesus is the Son of God
and that such faith sets us free
and redeems us from the fate of Hell
has created a wall of fear in me
— based upon the ambiguity and hotly debated
issue of which theology and truth
is the right one.

Downed Wall

I have not the right to interfere with your pursuit of God, but I do have the right to protect myself from you and your condemnation of me for believing differently from you; likewise, you have the same right to protect yourself from me.

I submit that God holds none of us guilty of anything, that not being a Christian or of any other religion or faith is no crime against God, and there is no punishment for having a faith of our own by any name.

Unburdened by Christianity, I now share my thoughts to add to the debate toward a better truth.

I will not burden you with the belief that my approach to God is the only way either. Rather, I submit that God is big enough to take us all into whatever is beyond this life.

I have come to believe that the opposite of intolerance is mercy and that the God in my heart is a God of mercy; in other words, I believe we all go to the same place after we pass on from this life.

I will continue on this path where the messengers are not greater than the message and where the message is that I can learn of God from my own inner reflections the same as anyone else. And without the burden to worship any being that others have turned into a God.

My fear of the wall rescinds more

and more every day.

now that the wall is down
come with me on this journey
make it your own

i am a layman and not a scholar
i am of heart, mind, spirit, and body
not a student of grammar or a
great literary expert
it is the journey i seek
and a faith of my own
i can chase.

Golden Rule Question

Do we need an intolerant image of God?
Is it possible that all scripture are only teachings of
faith the writers were willing to believe?

Is it more than likely that God has written no such book
. . . and insisting that God has done so is what
builds the kind of walls I have now torn down?

Could we learn to value each person as a creation of God
without any of us having the privilege to judge anyone
as God would judge?

Could we learn to be more concerned about treating others
how we want to be treated than how we choose to believe
or not believe in God?

The Quest

there is no wall for me now
    my quest is more true
the message of Jesus trumps the messenger

    worship the messenger? i think not
though looking in that direction for guidance is good
    but i do not worship the messenger
is it enough for Jesus to be a bridge to God
    as a messenger only?

what is it that makes our spiritual quest for God valid?

is treating one another as equal in value to ourselves
    enough of a message to heed
or do we also have need to make messengers
    into deities as well?

what is God's relationship with us?
    — my wall is down
    i am now ready to seek.

Lost and Found

1.

I lost heaven and hell as a choice
I lost hell forever
I lost reward and punishment as God's relationship to us
I lost the book written by us from God
I lost the one and only true way to God
I lost all human deities
I lost the intolerant God.

2.

I found a God who treats all humans the same
I found a God who does not have to punish any human
I found a God who belongs to no religion
I found our behavior on earth toward each other to be the
point of our relationship to God
I found God accepts us as we are, His Creation
I found many messengers
Christ was one of many.

3.

I found a silent God
who took upon Himself the flaws He had created
where none is guilty for what He has made
I found that our flaws are God's problem to solve
therefore God's mercy is His own redemption

I found our writings are our own
and are as offerings to God
for if God were to write a written word
it would be understood by all similarly
without question or doubt or arguments among us
as to what it means
therefore I found the virtue in a silent God.

I found healings and miracles happen to all people
of all beliefs—and that God is not exclusive or partial here.

4.
I found questions are supposed to be lights to lead us
So where do we go from here?

Note on Rainbows

to believe in a "great commission"
to convert the world to your belief
to believe that any human becomes or is God
to insist your belief is the exclusive way to God
— one that ensures that all your earthly and heavenly
problems and prayers will be answered —
is like chasing a rainbow that cannot be caught

though the chase is elusive
we are led by the rainbow to believe
that one day we will catch it anyway.

Chasing Rainbows

1.

i have chased rainbows for so long
that i have forgotten my way home

will i find a way back again?

2.

i sense the path i am on now
will lead me home again
my journey from here is like
looking for the way
that will lead me
back home.

3.

rainbow chasing is behind
me now and i can see
much better the road
that will lead me
home.

We Have This All Wrong

autumn sun so clean
morning light so quiet

the trees are bare
the air is still

this time of day
the colors of dawn excite my insides

   all seems well

but a new thought
has arisen in me and prevails

as i go deeper inside
i feel i know we have something all wrong

as i drive to a morning Christian bible study
the joy of the morning sunrise disappears

as i approach the door i know
that most of these men only want to hear
what agrees with them
— that any inquiry into why our beliefs are
what they are
will spark a fire in them and a response to
speak louder and to express their doubt
of my own salvation.

Long Time Coming

this has been a long time coming
and the thoughts run deep inside me

it is a mix of anger passion grief
    and joy
for what i see in me now is beginning to form
    into words
words that have taken years to coalesce

only now are these thoughts forming into a language
i already know so that now i can put them to paper

i could never admit why
many of the promises of the gospels do not come to pass

i could never admit why
the interpretations of this bible were so many

i could never admit why
the bible causes such rancor among us
and why the meaning of the words are so vague

. . . why everything is left so open to debate
leaving us to argue over meanings
of prophecies parables and teachings

. . . why we never allow ourselves
to question the bible's ultimate truth
or whether it represents truth about God

. . . and why we see nothing wrong with dividing
ourselves from ourselves over our disagreements

thus this has been a long time coming

How to Be Alone

my christianity has traveled so far down the road
of theology, doctrine, creed, and worship
that i have forgotten how to forgive

and now i am alone all the time.

Chasing Rainbows (2)

i have chased the promised theologian rainbows
if i persist i will surely lose the real meaning of
the relationship between God and me
for as i chase one rainbow others appear
and the chase becomes ever so elusive

is not everyone chasing rainbows?

Concerning Rainbows

One rainbow is as good as another
It is in the seeing and choosing to chase
that the excitement comes
Though it may never be caught
we can still say we have chased the rainbow

No harm done if the chase is for oneself
but what about using the rainbow as a pulpit
as "the one and only true rainbow"?

If all theologies are as rainbows
then we are all chasing one sort or another
and tempers flare when our own is threatened
Guilt is heaped upon guilt, as if our righteousness
increases when we refuse to abandon our rainbow

Enjoy a rainbow for what it is —
pursuit of mysteries and truths —
not to be claimed as a prize we have caught

Chase the rainbow if you will
but know that we may never really know
Understand that each of us needs to give permission
to others to chase their own rainbows
without condemnation

Perhaps all rainbows are the same in this light
Perhaps one is as good as another.

Life after Death

The darkness turns into a tunnel with light at the end
I am looking down on those watching me pass on
I can reach down and touch them but do not

> *— is this the God realm, where God can touch us*
> *but does not?*
> *— have i entered into the spiritual realm?*

This testimony is all too common across culture, time,
belief, religion, and so on and so on

The thought of what is beyond death's door
I contemplate here as it plays a role
in my inner exploration

Only those who have experienced the same
can speak of it with assurance
for those of us who have not have only our faith
and no proof

Facing death without prior knowledge of it
without an explanation from God
— the only real proof is in the dying . . .

> . . . leaving me to conclude that God is in control of
> life after death absolutely
> . . . that we are not held accountable for how we
> believe in God
> . . . that in that silence I can find a peace that requires
> me not to fret overly much
> . . . that God has left us to decide our own destiny
> while on the earth

And yet God decides what is beyond death's door
and chooses not to share that knowledge
instead leaving us with clear knowledge
of the rewards and consequences of our behaviors

No, God is not silent concerning that

But as to the judgment imposed after death
God's silence is again all too real
So we are left to the conclusion
that the mystery is God's alone
and the decision as to where we go after death
is God's alone

To trust in the silence of God in this matter is our's alone.

Part Two:
Openings

Character

1.
falling falling falling i was
in a dream with
no bottom

days without end
eternity without
definition

believe this way
they say and
you will get
there

> *then one day i slowly*
> *began to learn how to fly*
> *and i never returned.*

2.
most are saved from falling
but i was saved by flying

> *what is God to me?*

> *it is me finding in me compassion*
> *mercy steadfastness patience*
> *peace truthfulness honesty*
> *courage discernment*
> *conscience and other*
> *spiritual qualities*
> *like these.*

3.

try try try to
get your belief right
and you will keep falling and
— missing life

submit yourself to that which
you truly want for yourself from others
— and learn to give it to others instead

where the only rule is that true character
is formed by the value that you place on your life
and on the value you place on the lives of others

perhaps it is there where life will not be missed
and you sprout wings and cease falling.

Cows and Company

while driving on a country road with a friend
this friend said and i quote
>	*though i need to be alone at times*
>	*i need someone to be with me so i don't get lonely*
>	*and though i need to have company around me*
>	*i do not necessarily need interaction all the time*

after which i blurted out as we passed a herd of cattle
—for it seemed the right response at the right time—
>	*yes, even the cows need company*

my friend thought the comment rude and uncaring
but perhaps from the cows' point of view
they might have enjoyed inclusion in the conversation

>	*though i have to agree with my friend*
>	*that i was indeed rude and thoughtless*
>	*to believe a clever response was in order*

>	*learning to be good company requires*
>	*some thought before action.*

I Will Make a Covenant

1.
line up body
line up mind
line up heart
line up spirit
and bow to
the living God

> *make a covenant with me, my God*
> *and i will live with the covenant we make.*

2.
make me a covenant where we know
there is no written word of God to us
only our written word to God

make me a covenant where we can trust
that caring about one another is as close
to God as we can get

make me a covenant where no life is greater
than another

> *make me a covenant we all can live with.*

I Will Make My Covenant with God

i will make my covenant with God
and it will take some time
perhaps my whole life

historically covenants have evolved over time
no doubt mine will evolve as well

is it we who make covenants with God
and is it God who waits for us to make covenants?

do each of us have a right
to make our own covenant with God?
if so, who is to say *one is right and one is wrong – you?*

if an evil is here
it is our believing
our own covenants
are from God and
others are not

– that is how i see it.

I Will See You on the Mountain

1.

You and I are oceans apart
Our lives are as different as night and day
Our bibles are called by different names

We look on each other with suspicion and fear
and try to resolve our differences of faith
through intolerance taught to us as if God wills it

We are as fools believing we are wise
    — to think that God has given us the real truth
and that all others cannot access it
unless they become like us
What kind of faith would give us the latitude
to force our beliefs on others
    — as if God wills it?

if we perpetuate these ways
it will be nearly impossible
to have friends or allies for
long.

2.

Can you and I dream of a different reality
where we do not have such an intolerance
and where we do not seek to convert the other?

    for as it stands now our image of a righteous one is he
    who makes it his aim to
    convince all to believe the same

    and who shows his loyalty to his God with a
    willingness to die for the cause?

Will there come a day when we cease to believe
that God desires that of us?

Will there come a day when we cease
in our conversion efforts?

Will there come day when we see that we are all
of the same God

And equal in God's eyes
where no one is greater than another?

Will there come a day when we see no single way exists as
the way to God?

Will there come a day when we see there is no written
word of God, but instead only our words that we have
written to Him?

Will there come a day when we see
that God respects none above another and blesses us all?

Will there come a day when harming others is anathema
and when instead we treat others as we want to be treated?

Will there come a day when the evil are so overwhelmed
that they turn from evil to good?

3.
in a vision
i saw a mountain
we were created to climb

it was the mountain of God
and each of us was climbing

whether conscious of it or not
whether we live a short time or a long time
we are all climbing

i pray we learn how to see each other in God's custody
how to help each other make this climb
and see good days along the way

i hope i will see you on the mountain
where we can rejoice together
because of it.

Is There God (1)

is there God?
i ask as if my question would arouse Him
to prove Himself

i ask as if my question would answer how
anyone would invent the thought of God
if there were no God

yet the thought that God is in me
is something that has been with me
from before my birth

therefore to me the proof of God is
that i conceive He exists

> *i would also venture to say*
> *that the way to find God is already in us*
> *so i will seek God there.*

Just Below the Ridge

Just below the ridge where we live is a meadow
Above the meadow is a narrow two-lane road
that follows along the top of the ridge

From the side of the road I watch a murder of crows scatter
from the carcass of a dead cat as a group of children top
the ridge from the meadow below

Unaware of the dead cat till they come upon it the children
screw up their faces in disgust and then look away

The crows meanwhile circle above – *waiting*

The children cross the road to gradually disappear
into their homes on the other side
and the crows descend once again upon the dead
to finish dinner

> *though we share the same earth*
> *it seems the crows and we are*
> *worlds apart.*

On Madmen and Prophets

Is a madman — one who has done no harm to anyone —
guilty of sin?

Is a prophet — one who gives out true predictions —
a righteous man?

How do we come to the conclusions of morality
concerning issues like this?

Can a prophet be guilty of sins and still give prophecy?

Can a madman ramble on forever and say nothing and still
be a righteous man?

Would you rather be in the house of a cruel prophet and
hear the future or be in the house of a kind madman and
be loved?

> *perhaps the kind madman and the cruel prophet*
> *both have gone into the unseen world*
> *and have come back with victories*
> *and defeats.*

The Frozen Ground

The frozen ground, bare and hard, was like my heart toward God, until I realized that I could not blame Him for my heart's condition, and that it was you and me I blamed.

It is you and me I blame for the lame teaching, and it is me I blame for believing it. But my blame has now gone for now I see that there is no light in blame.

I am not guilty before God for being born. And if I were, why would God make you the guardian of my soul? It makes no sense in my heart or mind that God would make us guardians of the souls of others, but rather that each of us is our own guardian and God our only judge as to what lies beyond death's door.

I walk the road of God as I see fit, for we each have to contend with our own belief regarding what God is and whether He exists — or not. Therefore, as I walk the road of God as I see fit, I cannot blame you for my fall or give you praise for my rise. My walk is in God's hand and I free you of that responsibility.

As the ground thaws and the warmth and light of the sun embraces me, I find a new freedom, for my spiritual walk is now between God and me. I will seek to do no harm and walk this road the way I see fit.

The Lesser Prophets

We are the bowlegged and cross-eyed prophets
with the belief that we walk straight and see straight
We believe we have the right to judge the lives
of any who will listen
    — as if we know

And when the listeners begin to stray
and when they see the contradictions
do the prophets curse them for it or hear them out
do they learn to walk straight and see with less arrogance?

Beware of the prophets who make boastful claims
and when their listeners stray beware even more
For these prophets will add weights of guilt
to the shoulders of the many
and strap them with false debts owed
to keep them from straying further
and running for the door when they see that the prophets have
turned into salesmen and judges in need of their money

These are the actions of prophets whose spiritual legs are
bowed and whose spiritual eyes are crossed
Pay attention long enough to recognize the signs
and then abandon them and do not return

confessions of the lesser prophets:
    i looked upon a mirror and saw a beautiful image
    i truly admired and
    i looked upon you and saw them as inferior
    — whom i would befriend only on those terms.

To Walk a Better Road

i am no better than you
    and you are no better than i

i am not more spiritual than you
    and you are not more spiritual than i

if this does not seem true enough
    then i suggest it is time to get a better mirror.

The Real Peace

1.

. . . imagine that you and i are children
and God is like our mother who has asked us
to draw our house
. . . imagine our drawing of our house
is our belief of God
. . . imagine Mother-God displays each of our
drawings on the wall with joy and pride
and each drawing is equal in her eyes in value
. . . imagine Her working with each of us accordingly
. . . imagine no one drawing is right
that God understands all of our drawings
and knows how to work with each of us accordingly

praise be to the God who has the Mother's heart
for all her children

2.

a friend commented to me that if he did not believe in God
so this statement would not apply to him
    – good point –

as i am not preaching this as a truth
but only as a reflection of thought

i said in reply
    then please add your comments
    perhaps you can shed some light i do not have
    if so i will amend my statement

but please give them to the Mother-God
that she may display them on the wall
i am sure she will be as pleased
with your comments as she
is with mine.

The Trail to Nowhere

the trail leads to dead-ends
when we believe our plans have no more questions to ask
and when we are satisfied with only one possible answer

likewise the trail leads to disaster
when we use diplomacy like a poker game
and believe we can bluff ourselves to success
or possibly draw a winning hand

the trail leads to blood
when we are quick to draw our bows
and let the accusations fly as quickly as arrows
with no thought of respect and no thought to pausing
or taking a breath before the arrows start flying.

The Most Dangerous Ground

1.

I know some people who treat the truth like a scorpion
    for they know the truth stings
        and that it is deadly for them

See how they stomp their boots on the truth
    truth-haters needing to
        squash it before it hurts.

2.

There is a fear and an outrage in them
    They fear the truth for it
        brings them to ruin

I fear and am outraged at them
    To know that there are people like them
        means no peace when they are around

For what I see as a protection and a shield to evil
    and a beauty and a peace to life
        they see as a deadly insect to kill.

We Care

if we care and
if we are human

— the paradox is amazing

at first glance we can all
be at our best behavior

— yet truth can be patient and wait us out

if we could change
the truth of life

— then we would have never been born or wanted to be

the ultimate sacrifice
is well said by these words

*— if i cannot have it then i will make sure you cannot have it
either*

the way to war for sure
is in these words

— my God is better than your God.

Wise Sayings for Fools

"It takes one to know one."

"When a friend falls, kick him—as a lesson in life."

"When afraid and suspicious pray as you will, then lash out for your own protection."

"It is a better wisdom, compassion, and righteousness when you have the leverage."

Pet Owners

don't trust anyone who is
too nice or too mean to his pets

the latter will value you the way they do their animals
the former will value you less.

Meaning

what do i want out of life?
what will give me meaning?

health
love
wealth
interest
friends
generosity
safety
longevity
quality
spirituality
nature
travel
peace
trust
experience
learning

so many options, so little time.

Great Claims

. . . concerning the writings of times past, by writers of times past, making great claims of events and experiences of times past. . . .

Awed by their boasting, and challenged to believe without evidence, we refer to these writings as mysteries of truth, something which requires us to seek out a hidden meaning to the events in hopes of understanding what we believe to be true.

As if the truths are hidden by God and it is for us to seek them out. As if it is God's will to play hide and seek with us . . . and our searching is proof of our faith.

We seek the truths of these writings with much fervor, therefore, never considering whether or not these writings are in fact true, and over time create our own mysteries.

I question my own experiences with the unseen world and the reality of it. Yet these ancient writers appear not to have done the same of their own spiritual and prophetic beliefs.

Fully convinced of their truth, questioning is now forbidden. Without permission to question and debate these great claims we become irreverent and ungodly.

Is it that most writings claim to be of God, and are so full of ambiguous and contradictory statements that it only proves that they are of our own writing? Yet, we attempt to impose these words upon God, as if such a style were purposeful, to make the content a mystery to unravel—as if it were the way of God.

Why would God confuse us so?

Lonely Traveler

1.
I am a lonely traveler in this land

As I travel I find the land to be cold and distant
I look within me for strength and comfort
I sense a presence in me that is willing
to give me what I need in order to continue

And this is how a lonely traveler came
to know God through loneliness.

2.
I was lonely and now I am not

So I sojourn through this land
on a journey of the earth and of my soul
Both must learn to walk together
to learn to listen and trust the other

For it is all spiritual
and it is all physical
and listening to both is my key.

3.
When I looked around i saw others

I saw that we all have the same needs
that we all need assistance
along this journey
So as I meet others on the trail
it is sometimes appropriate to ask
how can I help?

Sense of God

1.
though i see nothing
    and i hear nothing
        from God

i do
    have a sense
        of God

and the sense
    of God is in me
        and all around me

God is here.

2.
there is no word of God
    only the presence of God
        no historical fact of God
            only testimonies of people

there is no Son of God
    or salvation or sin of man known
        and saying a thing is true does not make it so
            regardless, we are mostly cruel
                and only occasionally compassionate.

3.
there is no guarantee that faith works
    though we survive by our wits
        and hope faith will work

to some who are willing only to believe
    in God's intervention
        and who will accept that as the only proof
            i say this:

i have a sense of God
    and the sense of God is in me
    and around me
    and it has become
    the foundation of my faith
    and the testimony to myself
    of the proof of God.

As I Grew Up

1.
growing up
i was gradually taught
not to trust people
too quickly
    — which as a child was probably good

as i grew up more
the non-trust issue
began to apply to
those who were
obviously mean
and deceptive
    — which as a growing youth was probably good.

2.
then things changed
and i was slowly influenced
to believe that anyone who
was not a Christian could
not be trusted
because not believing in Jesus
meant it was impossible
to be worthy of such trust

. . . and then it developed that
anyone who did not adhere
to my own church's doctrine
could not be trusted
. . . and then anyone within the church
who was not a part of a certain group

could not be trusted
for the divisions divided
    – this was not good.

    3.
when there is no crime or proof of evil
but only differences of belief in God
when we insist that anyone who does not believe
in God a certain way cannot be trusted
because they are not capable of
trust as long they do not
conform to our beliefs. . . .
    – then this is definitely not good.

Bulls and Beliefs

The ministers cheered themselves
and said, "we penned the bull in
though it was wild and unmanageable. . . . "
    — it is our faith they were talking about

So I have to ask:
if my faith in God is compared to a bull
shall I view the theologies and doctrines
that impose upon us an intolerance of
any belief other than their own as the pen?
Shall I accept that the minister's goal is to subdue
faith as if it were a wild bull?
    — to them our faith without a pen is unmanageable and
    therefore sinful

Does it mean that the "calling" to be a minister of the word
of God is based on the belief that all bulls need to be
penned in, and that the minister is like the roper and the
church the pen ?
    — in other words, is the calling to be minister the calling
    for them to be lords of our faith?

Perhaps
I have a say in all of this
for it is my bull and it is my faith
and I will let it roam where it will

I say be content to pen in your own faith
if you so choose
and make it not your mission to pen
in the faith of others

the way I see it
if my bull is not free then it soon ceases to be a bull at all

but if you want your bull penned, then by all means
allow yourselves to be penned

but for me — my bull will remain free for there are
some bulls that must roam.

I Believe

1. I believe there is . . .
no one way to God
and no exclusive personal healing, visitations,
supernatural guidance, and intervention in our lives

though we have stories and true testimony
God does not reveal the source or why
all encounters and supernatural events show me
that their mystery causes us to point to a God
where all beliefs are accepted.

2. My view . . .
of righteousness is that
when anyone reaches out for God

God counts the act as righteous
and the act of reaching out to God
is the faith to righteousness.

3. I believe that . . .
the one-and-only-one-way-to-God belief is the fuel for
most of the division and wars among us and that it is the
false righteousness in which we cloak our faith.

believing in an infinite number of paths to God
is the beginning of knowing God.

Another Thought

1.

why would God need us to worship Him or Her?
God needs nothing from us
we need everything from God

> *i risk to say*
> *that based on the silence of God*
> *there is no thing God*
> *requires of us*

all we can do is acknowledge His existence
to seek within us a way to live on the earth
to make peace with our neighbors family and friends
and war as little as possible.

2.

though i am at peace and want not
to war with my neighbor it does not
mean my neighbor will not want
to war with me

> *so when is it that a person who proclaims*
> *peace must pick up his weapons against*
> *his neighbor?*

A Friend Said

a friend of mine said
that i have walked away from God
because i do not see Jesus the way he does
he says he will pray for me
and for my return

he says the bible is clear about this
and he understands it and i do not
he says i am doomed
because i disagree with the belief
that Jesus is the Son of God

> ... and this is my friend speaking
> whom i have known for over two decades
> with whom i have shared many things
> including trust and respect
>
> i have not ever betrayed that friendship
> yet now because i see these beliefs differently
> in his mind i am bound to hell
> if i continue believing
> the way i do

... and so our friendship's mutual respect and trust
has ended over this issue.

Journal Excerpt (1)

I love all kinds of religious buildings and sanctuaries and love to hear the testimonies of many cultures of times past and present where such sanctuaries functioned as a place where the community could seek God together. These sanctuaries represent to me a truth about our inner instinct to reach out to God.

However, I also see these buildings as places where men teach and promote intolerance and evangelical imperialism; to me, that is the evil of the need for these sanctuaries.

I believe the good in us seeks to be compassionate and tolerant, and that the evil in us preaches an intolerance for any who believe differently; so it is that I see both the beauty and the tragedy of our spiritual buildings.

It seems we seek to understand the good and evil in ourselves through our spiritual beliefs and that we search to know why there is good and evil in us, creating theologies, doctrines, and communities of all spiritual endeavors to solve the puzzle. Yet, universally, we have never been in agreement as to how this duality of good and evil can be cognized.

It also seems that God remains mute in terms of correcting this duality.

Are we to blame for the duality of our own characters of good and evil? If the Creator made us and we are flawed, then is it possible He is to blame? If so, God would surely not hold us guilty for any wrong deed or action we undertake or any belief we may have—and it would seem that our flawed lives are God's problem and not ours alone to solve.

And so it is through this thinking that I have come to believe in what I call the "mercy of God," and it is through that mercy that I have come to believe that we all go to the same place when we die. And hence, the idea of the intolerant God has faded from my consciousness.

Furthermore, if the silence of God is evidence of the mercy of God, then is our fate already determined . . . and our flaws God's problem?

Since my wall is no more I give myself permission to make inquiries such as this.

Journal Excerpt (2)

The quantity of believers
and the many cathedrals
do not hide the failure
of our beliefs
so I submit that at least
we could all admit
these failures
and not be so insistent
upon hiding them
by building more cathedrals.

Part Three:
Offerings

One with the Great Spirit

the drum beat loud
and then soft

the chant was the same

and the rhythm of the feet
moved in tune
with the drum

the great spirit was invited
to join in
and that was all that mattered

– *to be one with the great spirit*

The Sun the Moon the Earth

1.
sun
moon
earth
planets
stars
galaxy
universe
man
soul
heart
mind
spirit
plants
animals
and God

enough here to capture the imagination as to

how
why
when
where
and what
eternity
time
life
and
death are
all about

and we fight
and we kill

believing it is
God's will
do the heavenly beings fight and kill also
or is it just us?

we sin or
we imagine sin
we punish
we excommunicate
we exile
and we shun

we write books
we invent
we discover
we cure

> *and on*
> *and on*
> *and on*

2.
we are what we are
no changing it
a universal theme runs through all our veins

> *we believe our beliefs are supposed to make us*
> *closer to God and give us a better meaning to life*
> *and that God created us in order for us to realize*
> *that we need to be closer to God*

yet there is no agreement among us as to how
this comes about

maybe we could start over and
reconsider this relationship
between us and God
make it simpler

    by not sending anyone to hell

maybe then
we could
enjoy
the sun
moon
and earth
and help
others enjoy
them too

      and on
      and on
      and on.

I Think of You Often

1.
I think of You often
    though I have never seen You
I want to bow before You
    though I do not know who You are for sure.

2.
Though I claim You have written a book about You
    the book is so ambiguous that it causes much
    argument
and there are others who claim they also
    have a book written by You
    and this causes even more argument.

3.
If I never know whether You wrote the book or not
or whether You make Yourself known to us
    I will still desire to know You and
    I will still desire to worship You.

4.
You are the ultimate reality to me
and the mystery of who You are
has a hold on me
and will not let go

Is the answer to that mystery
the answer to the mystery of us?

5.
I would give up everything
to glimpse You for only
a moment

I would be as Your slave
if only I could be sure
of Your voice.

6.

I am compelled to seek an answer till I die
or till I hear otherwise.

However, in that search I will not let it steal my life
or deprive me of any joy I may have
for the silence of God in this matter
gives me peace to search
according to the dictates of my heart
and to be at peace
with what is answered
and not answered.

The silence of God justifies
me to live life to the fullest
as I see fit

And I think of You still
though I have never seen or
heard from You
– You are here.

Some Believe in Candles

some believe in the power of candles
some believe in the power of raising hands
and others in the power of loud prayers

    i believe in You

there is no candle
there is no hand raised or loud prayers
that will show the world what i believe

    only the way i live my life

if i light a candle
if i raise my hands
or offer up loud prayers
it is only that and nothing more.

We Are Like Children

we are like children showing our coloring books to
Mom; each and every coloring book is special to her

she accepts each one with love and approval
and with an understanding that it is how we see
the earth and the heavens

she displays each of the pictures
knowing it represents our needs and strengths

she works with us through the book
blessing our work and ministering to our needs

no one and no coloring book is turned away
for God is a mighty God
and is able to work with each one.

After Everything Said

1.

After everything in this work is said, I believe I will still worship the God I know in a form that suits me. . . .

I cannot be too critical of anyone's approach to God or of anyone's definition of God because I believe the distance between us and God is great enough for us to allow others to worship as they see it.

> *None of us knows the whole of it for certain.*

2.

After everything is said I go to my own form of prayer and seek guidance from God there. . . .

I walk in a way so as to not to judge others over their approach to God
and not to view mine as more right than theirs
or to convert them
but rather only to have the right to worship as I see fit.

> *What has judgment solved for us in this matter?*

3.

After everything is said I know that most of us want our version of God to rule. . . .

Just beyond the hill and down the path
we all always find a fight going
as to whose God is greater.

> *Why must it be?*

I Must Make this Note Here

1.

A friend of mine asked me once, "Why do you continue the fellowship with that Christian circle if you have a grievance such as this?"

I suppose it is because I believe it is worth the debate.

2.

Why is it we always divide and conquer ourselves to our own harm? After everything is said, I am not ready to divide myself from Christians, for I once considered myself one. But I admit my definition of the word is so different that it is as if I were never one of them at all, by their definition anyway.

I Take My Beliefs

I will take my beliefs before God and bow down
Whether God be He or She or neither
I will bow still

I will lay at the feet of God
Who I am and what I believe
comes with me

No one can pronounce me guilty before God
neither doctrines nor beliefs nor people
Only God can proclaim me guilty
and that is between
God and me

God has given me the blessing
to walk in my belief
and not be strayed by anyone

My walk is mine own
between God and me

I surrender myself to God
and to God alone
I surrender myself
not to any other being or entity.

Comment on Free Will

failure is an option
that comes with free will

if free will is a blessing from God to us
then with the blessing of free will
also must come the burden of free will

we are free to get a lot of life wrong

so what does God do with failure?
i would think that the God
who gave us free will as a gift
would also give us mercy

to go along with it.

Comment on Why Free Will

... Why would God create such creature as we and give us so
much freedom to do as we will and then be so silent as to why we
are as we are?

... Why is God silent as to his intentions? And why does He
leave it up to us to imagine what His intentions are?

— "why," being the infinite question, goes where it will.

Hell on Earth

1.
the only Hell i see is the hell we made on earth
which is ours to unmake

is faith the walk that seeks to undo the hell we have made?

may i have the wisdom
— *not to insist on a Hell we do not know.*

2.
if there be another Hell besides this one
then it is a hell in which no one can demand
our obedience by "saving us" from such a fate

there is no ritual on earth we could perform to right the
wrongs we do

why would God need a place like Hell
what need would be satisfied by punishing us eternally?

3.
why do we imagine God has created the world like this?
what need would He have to create us as we are
and then put us through all this just to satisfy this need?

i think it is better to follow the teaching
— "treat others in the way you want to be treated" —
— *rather than be preoccupied with a place like Hell*
or Heaven after death.

If the Earth Has a Prayer

does the sun enjoy our waking and sleeping
as we do the sun's?

do other beings on other planets
have questions like ours?

why are the flowers in the field
more durable than we?

why do the animals not form governments
or make enemies or invent?

> *— we do not add to the glory of the earth*
> *— we are the problem*

we bow to gods and esteem ourselves
righteous for doing so

and yet we gradually destroy
everything in sight

our worship of our God has not in any way
resolved our destruction

> *if the earth is a living entity*
> *and if it has a spirit*
> *then the earth has a prayer*

> *— and i think earth prays for us to be gone.*

My Soul Is Stilled

my soul is stilled

the quarrel within me has been silenced
and i am a more sure traveler now

the days do not bear upon me a weariness
i have bowed before my God
i am as an offering

with me come my own beliefs doctrines and theology
i lay it all at God's feet
as do we all, and wait for approval

i use my beliefs and doctrines and creeds
as a guide for my journey
and in that way it is as if i serve the God that is in me

the quarrel has left me
for i now see
my beliefs come from me
my own reflections of God
and i take them to God as an offering

my soul is satisfied
my soul is stilled.

Baggage

Notes on the subject of the baggage of yesterday

A woman gave a testimony as to how the burden of "yesterday's mistakes" caused another person to show her compassion.

She said that without yesterday's mistakes and without her carrying them around like baggage she would not have met this wonderful person who helped her solve her problem.

Though this woman regrets her mistakes, she says is grateful for the compassion of this other person.

It is a mystery how the mistakes of others can lead to a blessing for those in need, and how wonderful friendships can be formed that would not have been possible otherwise.

Questions and Concerns

1.

the portals of my soul
are as open windows
the cool breeze flows through
the night is restless
and the spirits of the dark are out

do i know God or not?
do i lay myself prostrate at his feet?
is it a pleading confession
or a strong profession of faith
that will make all things right between
God and me?

the songs of the dark spirits are in full chorus
i must dull the noise of their song
coming through my window

will God shut my windows or will i?
does He blame me if i do not
or do i blame Him if He does not?

this truth is needed now
for if i get it wrong
the songs of these
dark spirits will
have me.

2.

where is the vision of God
that can battle in a true way
for is not all life in the
physical realm?

why are You silent, God?
is all mankind redeemed regardless?
then why speak at all?
is your silence approval
or is it up to us to decide right and wrong
and then to fight for it?

why keep us guessing and fighting
and creating a word called "faith"
— to believe in God without proof
and to bet everything on it?

why do You allow us to believe that
You hold us liable if we get it wrong
and that if we do is all lost?
why keep us here like this?

what need have You of arranging our lives?

till better answers come
the portals of my soul
will remain as open windows
the night is restless
and the spirits of the dark are out
— haunting me to believe i was born guilty and fallen
and causing me to doubt an all-merciful God.

Where Is the Peace

1.
where is the peace?
— we pretend we know

if i win, do i have the peace?
if i submit, do i have the peace?
if i die, do i have the peace?

— is the salvation of man all about the peace?

2.
we lie
we steal
we murder
we create laws
we impose morality
or liberality
and we tax ourselves
so, where is the peace?

— is the peace the promise of an afterlife where there is no want?

3.
how about peace now —
is there a peace for the present?
though my outside man decays
does my inside man live and breathe forever?

— maybe that is the peace

and yet still
i wonder what we are doing here

as if some greater plan for our life
were being planned for us without
our permission

and as if the mystery of it all
is supposed to bring us peace

or is our reason for being here
not to know
and not to have control?

> *— and is accepting that reality the peace . . . or do i look*
> *elsewhere?*

4.
family
friends
children
husbands
wives
lovers

walls
open air
locks
no locks

routine
no routine
work
rest

fun and games
passion
learning

health
wealth
travel
fame
solitude

> *— is the peace in these or all of these*
> *or do we choose our own peace?*
> *if we do, then is peace a choice?*

5.
is there a heaven
or is heaven imagined?
whichever it is
then is the belief in heaven the peace
or do we die and then
... nothing?

is nothing the peace?
if it is, is the peace left up to our imagination?
perhaps that is going too far
but if you have not found the peace
then is it time to look further inward
or outward?

6.
is the peace like a relationship where it becomes a god to us
— where we submit to it and become a slave to it?

are we to seek after it like a god and yield to it
— is there nothing like the euphoria of the peace?

when it comes upon us it truly passes understanding
and its realm is beyond mind and emotion
— it is of the spirit.

7.

the elusive peace
though we claim it at times
and pretend it exists
can be like the rainbow
that cannot be caught or possessed

yet i believe that
if we seek the peace inside
God will direct us
not to chase that rainbow
for it cannot be had in the "chasing"

— perhaps the peace we seek waits for us at the door
of our passing.

Agents of God

1.
Are all the messiahs eternal agents of God
and all equal in stature . . .
  — *where all can seek them in their prayers*
  and ask them to make their petitions known to God?

It would seem so
for their testimonies are full of
healings, miracles, and visions
whereby their messiahs play an important role
yet all are from different backgrounds, cultures,
religions, and times.

So it would also seem
that there are many messiahs
none of whom holds a higher place than any other
and that all these testimonies
  — that name all these messiahs — are equal
believing these messiahs
have answered their prayers.

Is only one of these messiahs the true Son of God
or are they all Sons of God
or is none the Son of God?

2.
Why is it that each group believes
there can only be one messiah
and why does that messiah have to be a god?

It seems to me that there is only one God
but many messiahs
  — *i cannot discount the testimonies of all these people.*

There Is So Much We Do Not Know

1.

There is so much we do not know about God, and yet there is so much we claim to know . . . and we risk so much of our lives on those claims.

But more than likely there is no one right and true way to God, and the doctrines that teach there is are dangerous . . . for such a view breeds evangelistic bigotry and imperialism.

Whenever we begin down the road of this belief, we take the written words in books with us. We claim them to be God's word, which does nothing but perpetuate intolerance and create divisions and wars among us.

Perhaps it is better to accept how much we do not know. Perhaps acceptance would help us better see and admit this lack.

2.

Perhaps it is more true to believe that God does not write with words, and to believe instead that God's word is in us already and that we can learn of this God by seeking the word there.

I believe an act of kindness is greater than any act of worship or devotion to stories in books that claim to be God's word.

My thought at this juncture of life is that:
   — *there is so much we do not know about God*
   — *maybe kindness is a better way to conduct our search.*

Zenist and Christian

1.

The road to God is as varied as there are points of view
so I will give my own concerning the equality of beliefs:

If on the journey on the road to God
Zenist and Christian bump into one another the
challenge to their faith will be evident

If I bruise from the bump I receive from you on the road
and blame you for my bruise, then this is
where equality ends

Is there not room on the road for both of us?

If we both fall from the bump and I raise myself up
and then help you up as well, will not true equality
begin here?

Can we agree to make a space on the road where we can
pass each other safely?

But those who do not wish equality seek to dominate
and then the road is not shared but fought over
thus, their journey can be described like this:

I seek to convert all to my way
I can only accept them as equal if they believe as I
My road to God is not shared.

So, how can Zenist and Christian live together in equality?

I say, if they believe they can then they can
for the road to God is big enough for us all
it is we who cannot see it.

Stark Reality

perhaps God owes me nothing
and perhaps i owe God nothing

how I see it is
God's mission to us is unclear
and our mission to God is also unclear

so, conclusions on this matter have to wait.

Maybe

maybe we all worship the same God
maybe this God accepts us all
and it is we who do not
accept one another

maybe it is we who make up the rules
and imagine a punishment for not
following the rules

maybe that is the most evil of acts
— to cause another to believe
our rules are from God.

I Pray for the Evil to Stop

i pray for the evil to stop
and for the good to prevail

the problem is that one man's evil
is another man's good

i pray mostly for me and mine
i pray for health and prosperity
        and peace and happiness

the problem is that the truth of this prayer
is in all of us

it seems that children and elders
can feel the pain of others better

which makes it a good reason to have children
and elders around.

Part Four:
Moods of Religion, Politics, War and God (1)

When to Fight

1.

Where is the morality of deciding why to fight and how to fight . . . or not to fight?

Where is the morality in the pride of being an overwhelming power?

Where is the morality in dealing with the deceit of promises we make to our enemies and plan never to keep?

If I determine an enemy, how can I determine how to fight the enemy — on their terms or mine?

Do I defend the rights of others when there is no foreseeable reward? If I do defend the rights of others, how do I decide when the time is right — or do I defend their rights only when there is a reward for me?

— moral reasons to fight or not are critical ones, boundaries set are not always black and white, and boundaries can change like the wind.

2.

Is it fear that others will do us harm that decides our action?

Is there an answer to this fear other than fighting?

Is there a better way to confront an enemy without the pursuit of war, or is the fear of harm content to seek peace in war as truth?

— the effort put forth for peace comes with a price perhaps the morality for war is found in the effort put forth for peace.

3.

Though it could be that our enemies do not honor our efforts and we that we may remain enemies and our compassion go unreciprocated

— an effort of equal respect may cost plenty
but with fewer lives lost it is worth the effort.

4.

What could motivate us to seek this new way as a political solution to our conflicts?

Are all the children of the world motivation enough?

Or if fear is our motivator here, then what kind of fear do we need to seek a better way to confront an enemy rather than war?

— denial is no path to this truth.

5.

A friend of mine said, "Why dream of something that will never happen? Just accept the fact of war and be willing to make the sacrifice it requires."

I guess the road of my journey is not for my friend, and I fear if I meet him on the battlefield it will be a true test of our wills, and that war will still reign as the supposed way to peace.

— so we are back to where we started
with the morality of deciding why and when
and how to make war.

When Asked about War

1.
I ask, "How much are you willing to sacrifice?"

The soldier says, "I would sacrifice my life to see the sun shine on my children."

— *war is not kind*

I ask, "How much are you willing to sacrifice?"

The mother says, "I would sacrifice my life to see the sun shine on my children."

— *war is not partial*

I ask, "How much are you willing to sacrifice?"

The politician says, "I would sacrifice *your* life to see the sun shine on *my* children."

— *war is not just.*

2.
Someone scolds me after reading this poem. He says, "How could you be so crass as to speak about politicians in this way? My uncle is a politician."

"Okay," I say, "I mean all the other politicians, excluding your uncle."

Then someone responds with outrage and says, "That is not funny!"

My response is, "Neither is war!"

When a Warrior's Heart Kneels

though my path be lonely
i am seen by and esteemed by my God

my heart is on fire yet i am cold
my destiny is righteousness and obedience

that which i hate is taught me by that which i love
i have no choice for my vision is my sacrifice
and my fate is as a sword

the crescent is my light that surrounds me everywhere
the east is my way and my daily prayers are filled
with my hope

my death is a declaration that Allah is great
my heart has kneeled and i am now full of glory

i go now
farewell to my family
there is nothing here to live for

when you see me again
i will have servants at my command
and you will have your rest in my tents.

The Want of Drink

1.

the want of drink is strong within me
the bitterness of the luck of others reigns in my soul
i am every man's fear whether known or unknown
i lurk there at the walls that guard the soul
and wait at the perimeters of the gate

if there is no one to guard the house of the soul
i enter as if invited in
whatever i want or suffer
so does the soul i possess
there is no psychology to amend me
and no therapy to heal me

who am i?

i will not die ever
though you may scare me out and keep a guard
for i could return with others who have want
of a house as well
i fear only the real authority and cower
only to the real demand
i know that God is like a parent who bears
the responsibility for how we turn out
and fare in the world
— though not all responsibility is the parent's

though you speak lies it is i speaking through you
the truth as i see the truth as known by me
my destiny is of my own choosing and you are my captive

i crave to keep from you what i cannot have
— so who shall come and set you free?

i am the bright morning star in my own eyes
i am desire unbridled in your eyes
and i have the want of this drink strong within me
i will supply you if you bow and seek only me
for all your wants and needs

who am i?

i have fallen from the highest places
and i walk your earth with power to war against my God
by stealing His creations one by one till the last of His
glory is lost
you also walk with the loss
and the want of drink is strong within you

you know not your God as i know Him
i have a greater hold on you than He does
but i will not be satisfied with your death
i have determined to take you with me
and then my fall will be complete
—and that which has caused my fall
will be yours as well.

2.
i wanted more for myself than God was willing to give
so i looked out and saw man who was without sin
and in need of a strong drink
i did not want to drink alone
and so invited the man to join me
—creation without mercy is the meaning of hell

so come and drink
and be not satisfied with what you have
i am the comforter for what you are missing
until you meet your end

come for we both have the want of strong drink within us
you do not know my secret
—better to have been born without free will
than to spend eternity at my table

　who am i?

may the Lord God bless you and keep you
and lest He intervene in your life it is lost
so what do you have to live for
that will be in comparison
to what you have lost?

　　3.
i see in you the want of strong drink
it is the gnaw of your soul
and denial is the faith you present to God
as if He would not know
so may the Lord God bless you and keep you
may He intervene in your life
for without Him be He angel or human
we are lost and with mercy we are found

i am the fallen of the creation of free will
that which God has given to the angels and to humanity
is cursed and can only be derailed by the mercy of God

　who am i?

God's destruction for me and God's salvation for you
is the mystery being revealed
and time will deal the hand
of mercy when it is
time

the want of drink is strong within me
we are the same, yet God has not the
same destiny for us

i am lost and you are found
God reigns over all
the power of mercy
has determined
my fate and
yours.

Clash of the Gods (I)

Thought one . . .

> *How is it that every creed has a command to convert others*
> *to its way and to believe this command is the will of God?*

> *there is a fight brewing*
> *as if the gods yearn*
> *for a clash.*

Thought two . . .

> *What does our existence do for God?*
> *Though we do not know this answer*
> *the feelings in me are real*
> *the questions are valid*
> *the days are unsure.*

> *So, is it that we create a God who identifies us*
> *as a special group chosen for a special task*
> *and that the task is to change the world to become*
> *like us in that pursuit?*

> *Does it also create the vision that we have*
> *the answer to life?*

> *Is it our mission and our calling to*
> *convert others to see the answers to life*
> *our way?*

> *Is it so important to create a God*
> *whereby we force ourselves into a fight?*

> *For others also have the same idea of a*
> *God for themselves, and we are their*
> *vision, waiting to be converted*
> *to be just like them*

there is a fight brewing
as if our gods yearn
for a clash.

Clash of the Gods (2)

i would not know how to contemplate
a peace between you and me

we clash our Gods against one another
with the belief that mine is greater than yours
and with the result that peace is only an idea

put to rest the fighting and insistence
that there is only one way to God
put to rest the belief that we are to police
what we call by name "the great commission"

perhaps then peace can come closer to reality

why does our nature leads us to a faith
that gives us confidence that we know the way of God
and we are the ones who have it
and are chosen to enforce it?

why do we create a command from God
that we are to evangelize and convert all people
and erase the existence of any other form of belief in God?

we are drunk on this illusion
so the clash of the Gods goes on and on
till at last it will bring us to an end

i am vain to think a word here will change it
as i have discussed it with some close Christian friends
who can only shake their heads at me in dismay
as if i have gone astray — a common reaction

if my God does not like your God
let them fight it out in the heavens

why would the gods need us to
fight their battles?

Why not leave us at peace on this
earth and stop us
from the dangerous game
we play?

Politics 101 and the Machiavelli Sickness

1.
the crocodile
is out to get you
that's how you see it

for your kind of fear will only recede
when all the crocodiles are gone

the question is:
who is it that you call the crocodile
— the catholic or perhaps the muslim
or anyone who believes in God?

and if you believe they are all crocs
your best approach is to plan
a preemptive attack.

2.
two men who fear one another
deem their fear just may engage
in war

and if they bring with them the belief
that God is with them only
then it makes the war crueler

political and machiavellian acts are
no match in war against those who
bring with them the belief that
"God is with us"

If The World Were a Dog

1.

Kick a dog when he is down
and the dog will cower at your command
if your leaders want you to cower they see you as dogs

Feed a dog when he is down
and the dog will obey you
if your leaders want to feed you they see you as dogs

Kill the dog
and the dog ceases to be a concern
if your leaders want you to soldier in their wars they see
you as dogs

It makes me want to bite them.

2.

"What do you want of me?" asked the dog of the man. "To
cower? To obey? To be killed? Or is there another want you
would have of me?"

The man had no reply, for the dog's questions infuriated him . . .
so much so that he kicked the dog.

— Why are leaders surprised when the dogs turn on them?

3.

I think I would rather be one of the dogs than a leader.
If you think otherwise for yourself then I will always be
cautious around you.

Concerning the Truths

in truth . . .
our truths concerning spiritual matters fill our
garbage cans
and all the while new truths are coming in

and new garbage cans are being put out
beautiful garbage cans with stained glass.

All Kinds of Engineers

1. *Conversation with a white social engineer . . .*

"What do you want to be when you grow up?"

"A social engineer."

"Why?"

"Because I only feel safe in a white world."

"On what do you base this conviction?"

"A belief that whites are better rulers."

"How in the hell did you come up with a belief like that?"

"Other races smell differently from us."

Are we like this social engineer – unaware?

2. *Confessions of a moral engineer . . .*

"I dream of having everyone believe the same things I do."

"Why?"

"God has given me every right and every means to make this happen."

Be careful not to dine with these moral engineers too often.

3. *The creed of an war engineer . . .*

"What makes you a war engineer?"

"It means I will ravage everything in sight. I will take what I want. There is no morality that has taught me differently.

"When buzzards
swarm i see victory

"There is no democracy
without the dying

"I thought with my conscience at first
but now i take what i deem is mine
to take.

"There is no virtue greater than winning."

"Oh. I have no more questions."

I fear those who war without remorse. I fear them because we are all their targets and their weapons have us in their sights.

One Iraqi Man

The dust at noon is always thick
I am crouched in the shade smoking
I am only one of many staring into the dust
    wanting to see my family
I am not sure how many weeks have passed
I am not sure how many prayers have passed

Green men in green trucks are passing daily
    through our village
They are pale-skinned men who believe
    they were sent here to be our saviors
Their music is always playing loudly

I am thinking that before they were here
    I knew what my day was going to be
I knew how to survive and I had my family
Now I do not know what each day is going to bring
    I may not survive, and I do not have my family

One of the green men in the green trucks said to me
    that he has prayed for this day — *and now it is here*
I did not pray for this day — *and now it is here*
Why would my God want to take from me
    what He gave?

My Cause

the questions of a true man:
>   am i willing to die for my cause?
>   am i willing to kill for my cause?

the questions of a political man:
>   am i willing for you to die for my cause?
>   am i willing for you to kill for my cause?

Born to Kill

seems God made us in a way
that we cannot live at peace with anyone
      including ourselves

if we are not busy planning domination over each other
then we are busy protecting ourselves
against such domination by others
either way we end up warring
      taking what is not ours
      believing it is our right to take it

      within our own religious groups we
      act against one another, "just trying to help
      our fellow Christians to see it our way"

      add to that equation our zeal for God
      based on the belief that we are to convert the world
      and that to do so is our primary purpose for existence

      what follows is a justification and a cruelty
      which for some odd reason manages to justify war
      as if it were in God's interest for us to war
      with those who see God differently
      and blame our disagreements on the fact
      that their belief in God is evil
      and therefore cannot be trusted
      ever

      this makes it easy to avoid all moral conflict
      and of course the cruetly of our wars
      increases greatly when our foes see us
      as we see them

      the problem is we mistake winning to be the solution.

I Have Come in Peace... Who Am I?

1.

i have come in peace
surrender
or else

you need my help
whether you believe it
or not

i am better than you
because i have come
to help you.

2.

i will stay long enough
until i feel good about myself
and then i can tell others how good i am
though i am not aware this tendency exists in me

i will pretend to humble myself
and believe it is God doing it through me
but i will not know i am pretending

i will lovingly insist
with guilt and fear thrown in
that you must believe in God as i do
because that is why i am really here
— to help you.

Flight 93

united
everyone
for a common
cause

different people
of all ages
and gender

education
race
position
work experience

single
married
father
mother
child
tall
short
young
old

united
everyone
for a common
cause

this plane
will not reach
the white house.

Friendships and Roosters

a friendship lost must be reborn
like a fresh start where none is guilty
and trust is learned anew

it is shaking hands for the first time
and wanting to know each other
without too early a judgment

is the past so horrible to you
that no new effort will be able
to erase the mistakes made?

how does renewal work without
looking at what has already happened
and knowing people don't really change that much?

> *the fighting roosters went at it*
> *claws and all*
> *with no offense done beforehand*
> *and after the fight it was as if they*
> *hardly remembered it at all*

> *but we humans only have to hear*
> *a harsh word here or there and*
> *we never forget*
> *harboring vengeance as if ready for a cockfight*

yet we will never be as noble as roosters
for they can fight and let it go
till the next match

roosters are not compelled to rule the world
nor do they have the pressure of deciding
whether there is a God.

Politics and Religion

it seems we cannot avoid mixing
our political and religious beliefs
for both define our lives and both are motivators for
making decisions that concern our lives . . . absolutely

we justify our wars with enemies the same way
mixing our politics and religion
as if they were one and the same . . . absolutely

> *separation of church and state is a hypothetical*
> *so onward Christian soldiers*
> *marching to war we go*

when it comes to war our adversaries plan
to do to us what we plan to do to them
and we believe God is on our side

our adversaries also have a God
who they believe is on their side

we are the same as they
let us not deceive ourselves about this

we will always mix politics and religion
despite what any rule, law, or authority says

> *separation of church and state is a hypothetical*
> *so onward Christian soldiers*
> *marching to war we go.*

Grievances

The real grievances of your allies and your enemies
may not always be obvious in the grievance stated

For example
A street thug may be bitter toward his dad,
but he is in the street mugging you

Every culture has its own manual for war
as to why they fight and when and what for

For example
"We don't know for sure but we think someone
has a bomb like ours so we need to take it away
by force."

Part Five:

Moods of Religion, Politics, War and God (2)

There Is Trouble

1.

there is trouble in the land
where truth dwells

is truth locked up forever?
the holy books of truth we have
are myths and stories
the people in the stories
may or may not have lived

we are troubled because we want the
myths and the stories to be true
so we bow to a God in these
books and we stake our lives on it

simply put: the promises in the book
have mostly failed
and the theology is at best a guess
and as to what happens after death we
truly know nothing.

2.

the real God remains hidden
and i am left to shift
and sort through all the stories
in search of potential truth

i am left with my own heart and mind and spirit
i am left with my own sense
to discover in me what is true

the stories in these books
are a witness as to what
could be true and false

i am left with my own spiritual experience
and to discern through the experience of what
i see as real and not real
i am left to make up my own theology.

     3.
there is trouble in the land
where truth dwells

we trust words in books
the authors wanting
us to be loyal to them
or find ourselves condemned

they want us not to ask many questions

though the stories are full
of reliable sayings and reflections
they are also full of unreliable sayings

so, what we are left with
is not knowing any real truth
except maybe of ourselves
always drawn toward a God
keeping the mystery high
and the real truth obscure

so how is it we are to live?

many have reflected upon this
and have come up with different answers
there is trouble in the land
where truth dwells.

4.

we pray so hard and long
and walk so diligently
and receive so little reward

what we are left with is faith
in a failed theology

some do not put in near the effort as others
yet reap rewards from God without merit
in the prescribed method for reaping

so i am left to seek in me what
i can trust and what i cannot trust
in this book we call the bible

the world falls apart under our theology of God
yet we do not see it that way
but rather as God's will

need we be so blind to insist
that our loyalty to a view of God
cannot be challenged
when the evidence of proof is so small
that we define belief as the proof
and not as the promises fulfilled?

there is trouble in the land
where truth dwells.

War Dream

1.
i dreamed one night i was in a trench with a rifle
i was praying for God to help me
i could see my dilemma was great

should i strike first and pretend innocence,
or should i wait till each opponent fires first before
firing back
and then plead my case before God with a legality
of self-defense?
where is my conscience and what is the truth?

these questions seem important to me
as i sit in this trench
do i die without a fight and
let my fellow soldiers down
or fight this day and seek forgiveness
tomorrow?
      — my Christian teaching offers no clue

must we decide this for ourselves?
i believe the answer is yes
— with no condemnation from God

i must take my chance
and trust my decision
fight this day and seek guidance from God later
and pray now for God to intervene on my behalf

war is a dilemma unsolved for many Christians
i will kill today and be loyal to my fellow soldiers
and hope a peace in me can rise to this occasion
do i ask for the forgiveness of my enemy with

whom my country is engaged?
— if i die by their bullets would i not want them
to be held guilty by my God?

i blame not God for wars
but i do wonder at His silence
and why He chooses not to volunteer better answers
than the ones we have come up with so far.

    2.
i woke from this dream with dirt under my nails
and was unnerved for some time
for it was not like me not to wash
how had the dirt gotten there?
— was it the dirt from the trenches of my dream?

in life we must face many puzzles
at times left to ourselves to deal with finding the answers
so i will not be harsh toward you for facing
the same dilemmas
i give you room to work out your own salvation
and if we meet in war and are forced to fight
i will hold no grudge against you if your bullets pierce
my flesh

i hope you can extend me the same.

Martyrs

If I fight not and am martyred,
does it not give you a right to ask
why my life was lost if I changed nothing?

Why would you follow me and trust me
and then watch me be martyred?
Is to be martyred the real fight
or is it an illusion of some idea of glory?
I see a long string of written history
that would have me believe it is connected
to receiving a special place in heaven

If I choose not to fight and am willing
to be slaughtered for my belief
and if I teach my children not to fight
but to be slaughtered,
is it for them I do it?

When is it right not to fight—
to allow oneself to be slaughtered?
I would say that I would fight until I was tired and
defeated
at which point my willingness to be martyred
would have been for something I was willing to fight for
as well

Did Christ die in vain—
or should we offer ourselves up as He did?
    how the battle rages in me . . .
does this mood of martyrdom that lives in me
have a righteous form whereby I am righteous not to fight?
Is Christ to be my example of why not to fight?
If so am I relieved of the responsibility?

I dare say I would still fight to defend myself or my family
... and as to what "defense" is ... it is my own conscience
I do not think Christ addressed this dilemma fully

Where is victory for the martyred —
who go at their own risk to die for what they believe in?
Perhaps it was a fight in them *not* to fight

As for me I will fight when my life is tread upon
for I am a life created by God
I will fight for it and take my risk whether it is right
to fight or not to fight
For the answer is not clear in any writing I have read.

Sport for the Gods

If all religious views and writings are from God and this
causes us to fight within our own religious groups and
cultures and with other religious groups and cultures
    then that in itself is cruel enough
    ... as if it were God's intention

    but the ambiguity as to the real truth
    is added cruelty on top of that

So we fight one another
insisting that to win the fight means eternal life
and to lose means eternal death

    this leads me to believe the people of this
    earth are engaged in an intentional cockfight organized
    by the Gods — and that we are merely their sport.

My Quarrel

It is not the person with whom I have a quarrel. It is the nature within us with which I have the quarrel, for this nature is called to create rituals, creeds, doctrines, and theologies to which we gladly strap ourselves and defend as if we know them to be the absolute truth.

We split we divide and we fight for these beliefs, defend them against one another, arguing that your beliefs are wrong and mine are right.

Add to that the belief that if we win the fight it will bring us to a peace, but we all know that kind of peace only causes more warring.

So my quarrel is with what is within and our continual repetition of the same.

The Right to War

Though there are ten who want peace and show respect for all people, there are always ten others who do not.

There are those who are peaceful and pulled into war with those who seek to fight; all beliefs are challenged in that engagement, so do the prayers of both camps reach the heavens?

what is God to do?

Imagining our view of God is right does no good; to insist on it does nothing to further peace in the world.

The oracles of the right to war are deep within us and as such are misunderstood. Why would the Creator give such oracles — and if He did not, then would not He deny it?

Our right to war against an enemy is part of our righteousness. If we have any quarrel with it it is like quarreling with our righteousness, where we take the offense personally. And so it is with every group where war is the usual outcome.

*the destruction we cause
is nowhere near the
righteousness of God*

*if man is born with this mood of war
and uses it as a way to battle fear
where the courage to do that is
esteemed by him as faith
and righteousness*

what is God to do?

Earth Prison

My fear is that we have no clear direction or agreement with God, and that our fighting is the fighting of criminals in a prison where the fighting has no end.

Have we been sent to earth to pay for crimes committed in some other realm or time? If so, I hope I can pay for my crime and be allowed to leave this earth prison a.s.a.p.

Cold Water, Pickles, Chocolate, and Heaven and Hell

1.
cold water is
like God
with truth startling
and perhaps
not pleasant at first
but the truth is good.

2.
we are in a pickle
if we believe
we are
the only right
spokesmen
for God.

3.
warring for peace is like
believing
chocolate is
the only
food that
matters.

4.
heaven is in fact
a belief we
know nothing
about yet
we want to go
there.

5.
—and hell
we know nothing of either—
it is where
we send those
whom we
think belong
there.

And Yet We Will Fight

the sun will rise
the sun will set
and a thousand poems have said it right

the days have always come and gone
with sure predictability
and most likely we will not find ourselves fighting
over a disagreement about the rising or setting sun

but two men who disagree in their beliefs about God
will start a fight or quit a friendship in a flash
some are willing to die for their beliefs and some to kill

odd how we know so little about God
yet are harsh with our opinions
and quick to anger over what cannot be proven
where the anger is proof of our faith

we act as if God is impressed by our defense
and that our attitude will encourage Him to answer our
prayers

> *a friend of mine told me i rile him when i talk this way*
> *because my comments tear down faith instead of build it.*

The Craving in My Soul

1.

the craving in my soul is deep
for my soul has discovered
a void that no one can fill

it is *my* void and
it is *my* quest
to seek out answers
with which i can live

i am on my own and search for my own answers
maybe that is how it is supposed to be
it is up to us to seek our own peace with life
for it seems to me
the higher powers are silent on these matters

why would i trust another for answers
when their answers might only work just for them
i will seek my own answers
on my own terms
therefore making me
a true believer in the answers i find.

2.

i overheard an elderly man in the waiting room of the
hospital as he answered a young girl's question (his
granddaughter?)
when the girl asked why we wait until we are dying to ask
questions to God —
    . . . the usual question . . .

the man responded that perhaps then is the best
time to seek
when we are ready to hear and when the answer is so
important—
    we all need a grandfather like that.

She Lies on the Ground

1.
she lies on the ground caked in dirt
her daughter lies beside her starving

how thin can a body get and still live
why live at all?
what is it that would cause a mother
to hope that life could improve
and so sacrifice herself
for her daughter and
hope the sacrifice
will be payment
enough for
her daughter
to have a full
and meaningful life?

while the men of power set forth an action
thinking it liberation and democracy
they are bringing to the land
they cannot see
how they ravage
the land and
starve the
people

how perverse must an action be before
we see its perversity?

if it were our land or our daughter
perhaps we would see it clearly
perhaps we would be more careful
with the power

she lies on the ground caked in dirt
her daughter lies beside her starving
how thin can a body get and still live?

> she lies on the ground
> we do not see her because
> we do not seek to see her
> for we seek a different "truth."

The Age of Peace

1.

The age of peace of man was before the written history
of man
It came and went in a flash because the thought was so
tempting that it even made the Creator blink

— From that day on it was a race for superiority
for the fall of man came when man imagined
that the Creator had come to him and given him
commands for no others
... commands for only the most special
... commands meant to enable him to subdue the world
and demand submission
all with God's blessing

> *if there be a sin*
> *it is when we imagine*
> *ourselves as more blessed by God*
> *than others.*

2.

Gradually those of us from every corner of the earth
imagined we were the ones to whom God spoke
And then overnight the wars came
and since that time have never ceased
while each nation screams *the Creator has chosen us*

Where do we turn when we ourselves are consumed
with that thought
and add to it that all other people are wrong
and that only we see God's will for humanity clearly?

Where do we turn when all the while the silence
of this Creator is so loud that it is as if we are deafened
by its roar and therefore cannot hear when it speaks to us?

Is the reason for God's silence to have us discover
the nature of God
and the nature of discovering God?

The Dilemma of a Poisonous Cactus

A man went to dig a poisonous cactus from his path.

Should he go around it or dig it out?

Dig it out, he decided, for he feared leaving the cactus would only encourage more cacti to multiply and obstruct his path.

So the man went back to his house, retrieved some tools, and dug out the poisonous cactus by the roots.

After the digging was done, the man resumed his journey, only to find just beyond the bend in the path many more cacti.

"What now?" he asked. "Do I dig out these also or walk around them?"

It seemed an impossible task to stop and dig out each cactus on the path.

The man knew he could not possibly remove them all, and that even if he did perhaps more would grow, and therefore the task would never be finished.

True Intentions

my shoes are worn
my bones are tired
the ground smells of
death

> my heart is numb
> my mind is dull
> from faking faith

> > i must rise and
> > fight this day for
> > a cause i do not
> > trust nor make

i am dead
though i breathe
and though i eat
i am not full

> > we have
> > invented a God
> > whereby the proof
> > of His reality
> > is conditional on
> > winning

i fear this God
will not protect me
so i must survive
by my own wits
and fake a "praise
be to God"
for others to hear

i am led to war with
a people i know not
are there those in their camp
like me
who do not
want the fight or the
sacrifice either?

i put forth a challenge
that the God
who brought us here
is the same God
we have invented
and not the real God at all

for to war as we do
means the war calls
for a God who blesses
only the winner

if we die in war
we are promised paradise
after death
as far as history
is concerned
there are only kings
who are heroes in war

— *the true intentions of a God we do not know?*

today i rise and fight this so-called enemy
and defend myself

if i live i fear the ghosts of this day
will remind me daily
for the taking of lives is not so easy after the fact

      — the true intentions of a God i do not know?

but until i do know or until God makes it clear
i must live out this day in this hole
fighting a war for men
who have invented a God
who justifies their cause
for the battle.

Another Way

we are not animals
we are not gods
we are humans
upon whom there are boundaries

animals have evolved and changed over time
perhaps we have evolved too as humans
though i doubt we were animals once
and that we evolved into humans

does God then evolve also
who says it could not be?
if all creation evolves
could it not be the nature of God to evolve as well?

i submit that we look inside
and be not lazy in the search
for i perceive God is here

all creation is part of Him.

Camp of Wolves

like a camp of wolves
packed in a cave
guarding its entrance

ready
to devour
you and their own
with a regard
only for themselves

>   *about their neck*
>   *the symbols*
>   *they represent*

>   *a six-pointed star*
>   *a crescent moon*
>   *and a cross*

like a camp of wolves
only welcoming
other wolves
like themselves

though each is welcome
if push comes to shove
the rule is everyone for himself

we are like a pack of wolves
— but real wolves are better
their theology agreed
so none takes offense
as they tear
at each other's flesh.

An Intolerance Practiced

Inside the heart and mind of a Christian missionary:

See how we minister to those who are in need
of spiritual light

We feed them we comfort them we care for them

We tell them we are here to help for the love
of Jesus Christ in us

We tell them who Jesus is

We tell them we are here to comfort them
both physically and spiritually

We tell them they need to believe the way we do
or they will be punished eternally

We tell them we are here because Jesus loves them
that God sent us to save them from eternal punishment
by believing in Jesus the way we do

So enjoy the food, enjoy the medicine, and all the other
comforts, for it is free

But remember, we are here at our own cost
. . . so what does that mean?

> *though their help is admirable and noble*
> *but the spiritual message comes in loud and clear*
> *that missionaries are intolerant of other beliefs*
> *offering theirs wrapped in kindness and comfort*
> *— intolerance practiced in the most kind way.*

Part Six:
All Roads Lead to the Golden Rule

The Spirit of Christ (1 to 12)

1.
Is it the message or the messenger —
which one is the light of the world?

> *is the light that the messenger*
> *was born of a virgin and the Son of God*
>
> *or is the message the light*
> *— to treat others as we want to be treated?*

2.
Does salvation mean avoiding hell
or treating others as equal to yourself?

> 3.
> *i venture now to give you my view:*
> *i do not think the man Jesus*
> *would want us to worship him*
> > *for such a man would also know*
> > *he could not be God*
> > *or be equal to God*
>
> > *He would want His message*
> > *to be remembered most.*

4.
Why would God have need for us to ask Him
for forgiveness for our lives?

Why would God have need to sacrifice a life
to accomplish any form of righteousness?
no form of worship or creed can replace or exceed
a golden rule

— the foundation upon which I build my house
God requires nothing more of me.

5.

i believe if Jesus
were here he would
tell you
> *that he is not God*
> *and God is not you or me*
> *no disrespect intended*

the message i bring is
from me to you

the same spirit that
lives in me also lives
in you—seek and
you will find.

6.

i am forever grateful for the life you gave
the message you brought
the price you paid
willing to proclaim it
to bring it without promise of
earthly reward

though it cost you life here
i do not believe it had to
be.

7.
i see a great meadow
where all the great ones of the earth
are bowing before God on their knees

i see Jesus and all the others
beside them, many unknown faces,
each equal in the eyes of God.

8.
Why would God have the need to make humans
into Gods, or the need to make Himself into a human?

9.
weep not for me, nativity scene
i weep for you, for you are
a mother who lost a son
to a cruel world

regardless of how or what we believe
or what we think of him now
he only saw the best in us

there are millions of mothers like you
who also have lost sons
to a cruel world.

10.
if Jesus means anything to me
it is that he saw we are in it together.

11.

some say it is Jesus
some say Mohammed
some say Buddha

we all want a reliable truth
what they found we can find as well
where they found it we can find it the same.

12.

where then is God?
perhaps in the message
and not necessarily in the messenger.

Power of Belief

Is it that . . .
the nature of belief seems to have a power over us, to move
us to do many things that we would not do otherwise? Is
there such a thing as a right belief in God?

Or is it that . . .
we have an instinctive need to want the power of belief
to lead us because we believe the nature of God is to lead,
and that we are the servant and so give it a power over us?

Whether the belief produces the results we are promised,
the servant/master relationship seems a more important
part of that belief about our relationship to a God, and we
would be hard pressed to let it go.

It seems that . . .
It is our nature to give our beliefs power over us, and
that part of our nature frightens me. See how we run to
and defend our beliefs without real proof — only faith — a
circular argument as evidence of the truth of our belief.

And the lesson . . .
Faith is personal. When we believe something to be true
our faith demands loyalty to that belief and we take it
personally when those beliefs are demeaned. Regardless of
how odd the beliefs are or how intolerant, when another
condemns our belief we rebel.

This is a very difficult issue . . .
To deal with all these beliefs and to find a common ground
where we are all willing to accept others beliefs as equal to
and as valid as our own.

How do we stop this competitive approach — where these other beliefs need to be defeated as proof of the greatness of our own?

Proof of Truth

Proof of the truth that we supposedly have the right belief in God is in the occurring of supernatural events that we expect to manifest in our lives; it is the premise that those events are unique to our belief that forms the basis for what the teachers of that belief proclaim.

But what if the supernatural events are not unique to that belief . . . what does that do to our proof of truth? Does it increase our belief by including any who have the same experiences or does it make the belief void? And if others have the same quality of spiritual experiences as we do, do we claim their experiences are counterfeit and blame "evil" as the power that has deceived them?

We continuously pursue these spiritual experiences as the proof of truth and continuously call other spiritual experiences that mirror our own a fraud. Perhaps they are proof to us all in some ways, but to depend on these experiences as the most important sign of the proof of truth of God in our lives is a risk, because we can never satisfactorily judge what qualifies as miracles, healings, or prophecy. I say they happen to us all in some way and that many of us have had such experiences.

But if we do not have spiritual experiences, is there a better place to look for this proof of truth of God in our lives?

Can we look elsewhere for the proof of truth . . . or are we stuck in the mud with this attitude forever?

I bring this one to the table . . .

To treat others as you want to be treated is a way to the proof of truth, for it produces in us a life that learns to discern equality, respect, and a tolerance of difference founded on that belief that none of us knows for sure, and a compassion that has the ability to fill many voids in our lives.

My proof of truth is that we are known by the character of our lives and by the saying, "Treat others as you want to be treated," for this approach can produce a character in life that can stand before any other with respect, dignity, and trust.

I challenge any to compare their "proof of truth" with this one.

Ten People

I have walked this journey as honestly as I could. What I find is what I find . . . and how I see it is how I see it.

Each of ten people I know professes a faith in God. Four of them are Christians, three are of other religions, and three are of no stated religious affiliation.

All of them have a keen moral sense and all can be trusted to be fair, honest, just, and compassionate.

The four Christians disagree wholeheartedly with each other on many theological and doctrinal issues.

The three of other religions see God and their relationship very differently and walk in the way of their religious views.

The three with no religious affiliation pursue their beliefs individualistically, and yet seem as righteous in their behavior as the others.

> *i esteem them all*
> *for they have either developed a character*
> *or come by it instinctively*
> *to live by the motto of treating others*
> *as they prefer to be treated*
>
> *they each have a different testimony*
> *as to how it is they arrived at that way of living*

. . . All of which causes me to pause and wonder, What is the point of God's "want" for us here?

Ten people have found it and yet all see Him differently.

Terms of Peace

the terms of peace:
lay down your weapons
    or perish
    by your own actions

the condition of the peace:
    treat others as you want to be treated
    or continue
    doing what you are doing
    and perish.

What Is the Lure of God

What is the lure of God?

Is it believing a certain way
so all your prayers can be answered?

Is it the idea of a book written by God
and in that book are all the answers needed for life?

Is it the idea that there is a power called God who made
you special, and that you and He can have a personal
relationship?

What is the lure of God?

Why do we gravitate to resolving the idea of a God?

Why do we instinctively seek a higher power
from circumstances that bring consequences
unless a higher power intervenes or guides us through
them?

What is the power in us that can give us peace
from the dangers in this world that we may face?

Is this kind of lure of God written in us before we are born?

Why the drive to resolve this issue of a God when all of
history repeats itself over the conflict?

The Morality of It All

i looked into my soul
and i saw
> my heart
> my mind
> my spirit
> my body

i looked into my soul
and i saw
> what i wanted
> not to happen
> not
> to be lied to
> cheated
> deceived
> oppressed

could it be that the morality
> for us is
> not to do to others
> what we want
> not done to us

i looked upon another's
> trials and i saw
> unwanted children in the womb
> and love affairs of the same sex

i looked upon another's
> trials and i saw
> no immorality at all
> only the trials endured

for it is we who are immoral
to judge trials like these
as immoral

i looked upon my soul
and saw
immorality only as the
unwillingness to learn
and to practice
treating others as i
want to be
treated.

Part Seven:
Covenants

A Layman's Lame Description of Religion

the right to form my own conclusions
the right to believe as i want
the right to form an image of God that satisfies me

though God a mystery
God pulls at my soul
a power greater than myself i want to know

if i bow or build altars
they are mine to own
if the God in my heart calls me to bow i bow

friend condemn me not
i am as you
seeking what no one has ever known

therefore i seek my own way
not wanting to speak out too much
for fear the noise i make will cause others
to want to dispute my belief.

On Covenants

Is it that God desires each of us to seek God and make a covenant with God?

Are there as many covenants with God as there are groups, tribes, nations, and people?

Most likely there are as many covenants with Him as there are people. . . .

To me, a covenant is a very personal commitment to God. Therefore, all people have a right to write their own covenant with God and to name it whatever they want.

My Covenant

i see me walking into a meadow
unused and unspoiled
i can see the meadow in my mind
    my heart and my spirit
i do not know how i see it
    but i do

so i walk out into this meadow
as yet untouched by human feet
    i am the first to walk upon it

i say to myself
this is the place i will build my home
this is the place i will make my covenant
    with God

what i see beyond the meadow is
a hill that guards me from my
neighbor

i walk to its crest and look towards my neighbor
my neighbor's land is not well cared for
and no one is stirring about doing the
    needed chores

as i look upon this neighbor a surge of fear
suddenly runs through my veins
what am i to make of this neighbor of mine?

but beyond this neighbor is another
with a lot well cared for
one i would want

i scarcely thought at that moment
that i could have all kinds of neighbors
some who cared for their land and some who did not
and many in between

i wondered what kind of neighbor i would become
and what circumstances around me would mold
my character

with this thought another fear came upon me
the fear of becoming what i did not want
to become

i went to my knees in prayer
and i searched for a place in me that knew of God
after a short time i was consoled
and so it was i walked into a new meadow
and said to myself, *this is the place i will build my home*
this is the place i will make my covenant with God
and may the years that follow be good ones

and as i set my footprints and hands
over this untouched meadow
i hoped i would be a good neighbor
and inspire others to be the same

show me how to contend with the neighbors who care not
for their own land and who look to take what is in another's land

so my covenant with God began this way
and the house i built was of my own reflection of God

there are always chores to do around the house
and the land always needs caring for

amen.

My View

Once I came upon a man on my journey. This man was barely conscious and lying by the side of the road. I proceeded to make the preparations to care for him and to make sure he was well prepared to continue his travels.

And that decision that day made all the difference in my life thereafter. . . .

Thoughts on Faith and Righteousness

1.

Some describe faith as a way that God provides for us to make, alter, and change events in our life for the good, and this becomes the way we prove God working in our life. Others describe faith as a set of beliefs and rituals by which they live.

One man in the Old Testament named Abraham believed he was justified by God by his faith in God. To me, it was that he understood that this word "faith" meant the ability in him to have the profound realization of the existence of a one and true unseen God, and that realization meant that God justified his (Abraham's) existence. It was the realization that God existed and that God was with him that became his faith and truth. This man's story is his testimony of how he saw it, and the record of it is how the writers of the story believed it happened. According to this man's reflection, it was his faith and belief in an unseen God that became the meaning of the word "righteousness."

I believe this man had hope that this God would be with him and available to him for all things in life that would arise, whether life-changing events or the seeking of God's guidance to know how to walk through those events. The important element here is that the existence of God was shown to Abraham by his faith and that faith was the proof of God, not necessarily in what he hoped this God would do.

2.

. . . If faith is the commitment to words and confessions
and rituals and creeds

> *then it could be that I have not faith*

. . . If faith is an acceptance of denominational doctrines
and theology

> *then it could be that I have not faith*

. . . If faith is the willingness to believe in a God I cannot
see
> *then it could be that I have faith*

. . . If faith can show us the realization of the profound
truth that God is

> *then it could be that I have faith*

> *. . . according to the man Abraham in the Old Testament*
> *i do have faith — and have become a righteous man.*

Covenant Makers

I am a God-believing man without title
I am not of any doctrine that I know
I am of my own making and
I am on a journey as you are

We all risk the submission to our beliefs
We hope that our beliefs are from God
So I give you room on this road
May all of us have a good trip.

The Illusion

illusions of the spiritual
haunt me

conclusions lost in a mirage
of belief

we cannot agree
on the unseen

my own image
of a God
> *leads me to trust*
> *only a person's*
> *character*
> *as truth of their*
> *closeness*
> *to God.*

God's Covenant

Treat others as you want to be treated and you will find Me there.

The fruits of the spirit are in us all to take and use.

God's mercy waits for us at the end of this life.

There is no hell, only mercy . . . and then heaven.

God does not reveal much about Himself to us.

Free will is a gift from God.

Part Eight:
Where to from Here?

Encounters with God

1.
the crowd was spellbound
as the young girl got up and walked
they watched as her disfigured back straightened
and then gasped in amazement

2.
the bullets were flying overhead
and there was no way out of the trap
the mother and her four children
hunkered down below the wall
and as the enemy troops passed them by
it was as if they were not there.

3.
the storm blew hard and the rain came like darts
the grandfather and his grandson were stranded
on a roof with no escape
then the grandson spied a lone boat
with a woman in it drifting aimlessly
then the boat hit the roof top and settled there
for a few moments
and the grandfather and grandson jumped in
happy to see each other
—she had the boat
the grandfather and grandson knew how to steer it.

4.
the group of ten were at their last hours
no food or water could be found anywhere
the elder of the group had wandered off for one last
try

through the dust storm he could see a caravan of
people on camels
he approached them but they would not stop or
acknowledge him
then suddenly he saw a bundle fall off the last camel
as it passed, and wondered if they knew
and had thus sent a bundle his way as an act of
compassion
or had God caused it?
—either way it was a blessing
for in the bundle were five gallons of water
and enough food for ten for three days.

    5.
the stories go on and on
and the people are from many cultures and religions
i was taught that we were not to honor any of these stories
unless Christ were preached
we were expected to believe
that people were spared tragedy or given blessings
only so they would hear Christ preached

    —our teaching on that subject is very embarrassing to me.

God Is Bigger

God is bigger than Christianity. Christianity could not and does not engulf the totality of the truth of God.

To me there is more truth in the idea of God as a God of mercy for all people, regardless of any and/or all theologies or beliefs combined.

. . . And a single act of kindness towards another is a greater worship of God than any religious doctrine creed or ritual.

So I submit that God is bigger than any theology or religion ever composed, and our behavior towards others is where the God in whom I believe is to be found.

I do not know the relationship Jesus has with God. If I call Jesus my Messiah it is only that he is my bridge to God, for the idea of a Messiah only applies to the sayings, parables, and teachings; a bridge is a bridge, not a human who is also God.

There is no real evidence, so why do we have to make humans into Gods and call them Messiahs in order for God to be real?

Lay Down Your Weapons in the War of Scriptures

One question:
What burden has God put upon us
to require us to war?

As I write this I see that the problem
with us *now* has become the nuclear
capability of our words.

The War Policy

When I have exhausted my pursuit of peace with my neighbor will my army be strong?

When do I know when to send out the army, and when do I know when peace with my neighbor has failed?

Do I wait till my neighbor has fired the first shot to know when to go to war, or are there other ways to decide it?

Can I correctly judge the consequence of war and whether I can win as the factors for going to war? Does my judgment then give me the right to fire at my neighbor when I am ready?

Or is my conscience a better guide, so that when I have become impatient with my neighbor my conscience tells me to fire the first shot? Are the consequences of my actions then only secondary?

Whatever the reasons we decide when to war with our neighbor, whether we wait for them to fire first, weigh the consequences and victories, or use our conscience as our guide, we must know that war requires our soul's coming to terms with what brings it to war.

Therefore, I submit that it is always best for us to exhaust the ways of peace and set the bar very high concerning the meaning of "exhaust," and to consider war the greatest of failures in the effort to make peace with our neighbor.

Sample of Nature and a Lecture

1.
i will bow only to the God i see
inside me and outside me

> *i am calmed by a breeze on a hill*
> *why does it calm me so?*

2.
i will not give anyone my earnings
who promises he knows
the promises of God
for me

> *there is something about a walk in the woods*
> *and the solitude and quietness of that walk*
> *that bring a quietness to me*
> *and that quietness far exceeds*
> *the request of any preacher*
> *to give him money*
> *in exchange for that quietness.*

3.
i can watch a flock of geese heading south
or see a herd of elk grazing in a meadow
or spy squirrels on the limbs of trees
and learn more of my belief in God than i can
by learning doctrines that teach me an intolerance
toward my neighbor
merely because my neighbor believes in God differently

> *why do i not go to the woods more often*
> *rather than to church?*

the idea of guilt can steal the soul before you know it
so i tell myself "run as fast as you can to the woods."

4.
i will bow only to the God i see
inside me and outside me

i am calmed by a breeze on a hill
why does it calm me so?

I Want to Serve You

i want to serve You and
worship You
but i know not how
for Your will
is not well known

Your silence is a mystery
our freedom to create a
theology of You the same

we are drawn to You
given the freedom to make
our own conclusions
with little help from You

> *as long as the unknown of You is part*
> *of our relationship with You*
> *then i must search within me*
> *to come up with what it is*
> *i am willing to believe in*
> *and then go for it.*

What If You Knew?

1.
What if you knew it did not matter . . .
> concerning the existence of a one and only true
> theology,
> or whether or not the Son of God exists,
> or whether or not any humans are deities from God?

What if . . .
> everybody goes to heaven regardless of belief?
> would we be fighting for domination of the world?
> would we starve and oppress others?
> would we be as selfish?

> *in other words*
> *would knowing this*
> *relieve a pressure*
> *that would cause us to*
> *respond differently to the world?*

2.
What if we all go to heaven . . . ?
> would we have a little more joy in this life
> without having to spend the time searching for
> the truth and carving out a lifestyle based on
> theologies, doctrines, and ideas of eternal reward and
> punishment that our faith leads us to believe because
> we do not know for sure if they are true?

> would we be more compassionate in helping others
> if we knew that we were here only for a while and
> then went on to a better life . . . and that all that was
> asked of us is that we care for each other and care for
> the earth for the next generations?

I Walk Not Alone

though i seemingly walk alone
i walk not alone

and though i know You not
i believe You are with me

Your silence is my assurance that
You require nothing of me
in order for me to get to heaven

and after my death
i believe You will be there

You have me in Your hand
though Your help for me
is not something i can make out for sure

it is enough for me to know
i am willing to believe
You wait for me in the next life

i walk not alone.

Message to Myself

1.

prepare me God
to die with dignity and unafraid

teach me God
to live with a joy and contentment

and in all trials and tribulations
victories and successes
show me the peace
that passes all these understandings.

2.

if i can enjoy the joy of my friends and family
despite my own pains
then i will know a kind of love that does not
measure itself by its own well-being.

3.

i am no man of the church
nor am i a man
who esteems his own doctrine
as the only true way to God

i do not know for sure what is after this life
i do believe for sure that no one else knows
these things either

i am no tither to men or churches
for the sake of relieving me of hell
if hell exists at all

i give all people the right to worship and believe as they
want without judgment
and i want the same right given to me

i object to beliefs that proactice intolerance of other beliefs
and expansionism of their beliefs
over the beliefs of others.

Sooner or Later / Sooner than Later

1.
take the quietness of the day
with all the beauty of nature

and then add the human species
and it spoils it all

sooner

      or

           later.

2.
though i do love some humans with all my heart
   — i don't love them all

and though i love most of the animals and plants
   — there are some with which i have a problem.

3.
are we to love those who don't love us
i have heard it spoken of by many religious groups
that it is possible and a good idea
to love everyone and anyone without condition
because it is the way to heaven

   — however, there is no proof of that.

The Good and the Evil

the good and the evil in us
are never fully revealed
or destroyed

humans on earth are the
enigma of the good
and the evil.

To Enjoy Life

to enjoy life one must have
permission to enjoy it

if all religions, groups, gatherings, sects,
or whatever you call them,
define joy only in the form of serving
them and their God,
is there another joy?

i think there is

. . . a joy in us we do not have to learn,
one that comes as simply and easily
as watching children play.

I Will Object

i object to any and all religious pursuits
that promote expansionism of their doctrines and
theological position
and teach them as the will of God

i object to any and all religious pursuits
that teach tolerance of other beliefs as sin

i applaud any and all religious pursuits
that teach ambiguity as to the "truth" of the beliefs
so that we cannot demean or condemn
or be intolerant of different beliefs in God

i applaud any and all religious pursuits
that practice peaceful means to resolve conflict
and adhere to a few rules and boundaries:

> *— to value all human life as equal to our own*

> *— the right and deserved respect to believe in God as one
> wants if it does no harm to others*

> *— the right to protect oneself from harm*

> *— the belief that God sees us all as equal to one another.*

What Is It That Has to Be Revealed

1.

can i love God
without the known biblical theology as my reason?
can i love God
without Jesus having to be the Son of God?
can i love God
without having to be redeemed for some imagined sin?

i can love God
for my own reasons and not adhere to reasons
that are not my own

my reasons are as valid as others
and valid for me
the point of my love for God is to learn how

— to treat others as we want to be treated.

2.

though we worship differently
and we pray differently
and our view of our relationship
to God is different

if we are equal to one another in the eyes of God,
what is it that has to be revealed to us
that will compel us

— to treat others how we want to be treated?

Part Nine:
Back Where I Began ... Only Wiser

The Way Home

how would i find my way home
after diverging from the path i knew
to paths that seemed good at the time

the key to it
— to me —
was knowing where to look
and how to look

i had to be alone for a while
and seek the quiet
places in my soul

and after spending time
— just me —
i arose from the
quietness and joined
others once again

it was there i tested the
new strength i'd found
in my search for the way home

i go there often now
to return to test my findings
among others

i retreat
i rise
i go back into
the world again
and again and
again

and so it is in the quietness
of my soul i go
to listen
and search

the path opens to me
leading back to where
i began
and when i stray
i retreat
to re-find myself
over
and over
again.

Concerning Pulpits and Their Owners

the way i see it

you have the pros
and you have the cons
then there are the rest of us
and many of us are the followers

some of us follow the pros
and some of us follow the cons
we have let them create theologies
and we let them lead us by their theologies

the good news is that there is God
and God does not have a theology
if we prostrate ourselves before others
it is our fault
so let us rise up and walk away from their pulpits

> *if there be a pulpit of God*
> *it is within us*
> *and i think it needs not*
> *these pros and these cons.*

I Think Of You Often (a love poem for my wife)

i think of you often
i think of you very often
i think of you so very often
— *i think of you while walking in the meadow*

one day i told that secret to a meadow
where i often walk
and the meadow seemed filled with joy
knowing that i think of you there

i think that is why all the flowers in the
meadow are there
because flowers can read our thoughts
and find joy in knowing that as i pass by i think
of you in their meadow

so i make it a point to think of you
while i walk through the meadow
— *all meadows*
believing all the flowers
in all the meadows know
— *i am in love with you.*

The Journey Back Home Was Good

the journey back home was good
i am no longer looking for answers
— only observing life

> there was a boy who grew up strong
> and a girl who grew up beautiful

> as all fairy tales go
> they met and married
> and lived a long and joyful life

> i have observed this . . . it does happen.

God Is the Greatest

god is
the
greatest
creation
of all

    creation.

Making Men

making men
into gods
is
possibly
the worst
of all

creations.

I Long for You

i long for you
    the nights are the most difficult
    for my mind is weary of reaching out to you
    and though the mornings wake me rested
    i still long for you

the scenario repeats itself over and over
    and i am not alone in this
        for others long for you as i do

it may seem here as if i were
    speaking of a woman or even a man
    but what i speak of is neither
    i speak of what i was born to do
    to seek after you

will you be forever aloof to me
    history bears your coldness towards us
    and yet we are unfazed

what could compete with my longing for you
    what is so great as you that would cause me
    to want you more than i would desire a woman
    and yet you answer not

if i could only once have but a glimpse of the real God
    it would give me all the comfort
    surpass all my dreams forever more
    and yet you remain silent and distant
        until at last i imagine you are speaking to me

the libraries are full of the same testimony
    of those like me who want you so much
    that our imagination creates a voice
    one we imagine is you

we are so enamored by this conquest
    that this fantasy becomes real
    so real in fact is our imagination of you
    that we become intoxicated by it
    so much so we believe it to be true

this is the greatest power of love there could be
    and yet there is no real response from you
    so why would you make us desire you this way
    why do you turn your head
    i would not accept love from any human this way
    as if we were not meant to love you
    in the way we love humans

what sickness have we entered into
    — as if the truth says seek me regardless

the sickness of my love along with the way i long for you
    provides no relief
    and you do not respond to my longing
    — i give warning to us to beware

for you will let us seek you as we will
    and imagine you as we will
    but *your* love for us is not this way

so how do you love
    is your love shown by your gifts
    is earth as your gift to us

and is a woman as your gift to me
and am i as your gift to her

so, how is it God loves?
    i must see it that way
    and not long for you in the ways
    that you do not show yourself

so, in your silence i must learn of you and
    your way with us
    i must see the gifts you offer and
    in what spirit you offer them.

so, in this way i must learn how to live with the true God
    and not long for a God that is not
    for if i wait for you in the way you are not
    then i will miss you
    and miss the gifts of life that you have given.

True Conversation of an Elderly Friend

The woman said, "And there we sat, watching the evangelist healer perform an act called 'spinal alignment healing.' This man asked one of our friends to sit in a chair and hold out her legs horizontally. She did as the man asked and then he held her legs gently, and as he did this he pointed out to us that one of her legs was slightly longer than the other one. He then commanded 'in the name of Jesus' for the right leg to extend evenly with the left leg. As I watched in anticipation, being very engrossed in the drama of the event, my mother, who is ninety years old, suddenly yelled out for the man to stop, for it seemed to her that the right leg of this woman was now longer than the left.

"The spontaneous laughter of the group seemed to erase the embarrassment at the man's so-called spiritual healing act. I have attended many 'healing' meetings and I never saw or heard of any close friend of ours being healed of any real physical ailment, yet it cost us plenty of money to sit there, for these healers know how to get to your pockets. And it still goes on today in the very same way. And I can guarantee you it is always all about the money."

The woman then added one last statement. "Show me a ministry that does not preach for the money or demand some kind of loyalty in exchange for their performance, and I will show you a ministry that could not survive — which may be what is needed."

To Ramble

To be willing to treat others as you want to be treated is the only relevant point of our relationship with God.

Why ramble on?

I Will Not Ramble

most of us do not want to be treated in deceptive and
harmful ways

so, for us to learn and be willing
to treat others as we want to be treated

could possibly be the only relevant point
that God has for us here.

One Liner

Is the way to heaven linked to our behavior on earth? I think not, for if heaven were linked to behavior then we would be doomed . . .

And if we believe that believing a certain way takes care of our bad behavior then we are doomed even more . . . for we argue and fight over which way is the right way to believe.

Could it be that we all receive mercy from God when we pass onto the next life? That would be good enough for me to want to treat others as I want them to treat me . . .

Solitary Place

1.

the solitary place i go in me is what i call my soul
it is where my conscience resides
the place where my heart and mind
connect with my spirit
to decide what is right and what is wrong

if this is so, then where is the anchor of my soul
where my conscience can be secure in times of storm?
where is the anchor for my mind and heart?
i say the anchor is found in my spirit
and it is there where i go to know of God
and to take of the fruits of God's spirit

is it there, where the rights and wrongs are seen?
it is there, where the actions of my life can
draw upon strength   courage   wisdom   and compassion
and discern a thing to be right or wrong?

if so, then it is up to me to go there and to find it
that is what God asks of me
but if i find it not, i believe God does not hold me liable
for the "not finding" it is no crime against God.

2.

i believe the silence of God
does not hold any of us liable
for God does not make it known
whether our actions are subject to an eternal judgment
therefore God does not make us liable
for not finding these truths

though to me it is worth the time to seek these truths
just for the privilege of knowing God here on earth
and i judge not anyone for seeking or not seeking
for the silence of God on this matter may be
God's way of saying that God is for us all
whether we are seeking Him or not.

3.

if one person goes to heaven
then we all go—God's mercy is not partial
and it condemns none.

Predicament

Why would God need guilt and fear
to entice us to serve Him?
That would be like a prison that keeps offering freedom
and therefore keeping the inmates on edge.
That is not the God I know.

Fear and guilt is not a path to God
It is the path of submission to religious leaders.

When we take back our freedom, the path to God,
guilt and fear cannot follow

It is we who make religious leaders
—as long as there are followers
We enter their prisons like sheep
yet we can walk out anytime.

God has no requirements for us to seek Him there.

Daring as It May Seem

Timid as it may seem, my venture to decide how I shall worship and approach God amongst a very defined group of Christian people who all agree more or less on how to worship and approach God is, in fact, to me, daring.

Since my deviation in theology and doctrine is seen by this group as an assault on God, I am therefore counted as one who turned away from God, and these people will spend time in prayer for my soul, when in fact it may all be wasted time.

For the time any of us spends in judging another's worship and approach to God is most likely wasted, as are the prayers we offer as if we are not judging. But it is God who does the judging . . . and for us to judge on these issues is most likely more daring than it appears . . . which is to believe we know how God judges on these issues.

see me as your equal without need to convert me
for i am a creation of God
and i have no need of your saving me

God and i are at peace with my salvation.

A Wisdom of Our Own

in a dream
the hand of God reached down
and it was a hand like my own

during this brief dream
this thought came to my mind
as if God were speaking:

> *each person has a*
> *wisdom of his own*

> *it is from Me to you*
> *— learn to walk in it*

> *it is your wisdom*
> *your gift, and it is*
> *unique*

> *a part of me*
> *given to you*

i do not claim these words are from God
rather i understand this dream
to be my own reflection

> *i see in this dream that God gives unique and special*
> *qualities to each of us*
> *and though there may be miracles, healings,*
> *and interventions by God at times*

there are also the gifts and wisdom we have received,
whereby we learn of God
when there are no miracles, healings,
or interventions.

Love Me: A love poem for my wife

as i walk the quieter parts of the trail
i am swept up by the solitude
of the beauty of nature all around me
but the deeper beauty of it all is felt
when i can share it with you

the sounds of birds awakening
the cool breeze of the morning
minister to my soul like nothing else
and yet when you are at my side
the birds awakening and the breeze
of the morning are even more soothing

i could never find anyone on earth
as beautiful as you inside and out
there is only one you
and i am the most fortunate of men
to have you want me as much as i want you

> *love me till the morning comes*
> *and then love me more when*
> *the evening sleeps and love*
> *me the times between these*
>
> *love me till there is no time left.*

Rainbows and Sunrises and Sunsets and God and Me

1.
i am at a relative place of peace now
about what i believe God to be
and why i believe in God

i do not hold anyone guilty
for not seeing or believing in God
the way i do

the way i see it is each of us has guilt enough
for the damages we do to each other
and the earth

i believe it is wise to have a conscience
that values our behavior towards each other
and holds the earth with reverence and compassion

for if we are all to be greeted with the mercy
of God at death
i would want to have some "show of effort" on my part
when He greets me

and though i believe we will all receive the same mercy
i still want to make a show of effort on the earth
to make it a better place before i leave.

2.
i saw a rainbow yesterday
it was in the late afternoon after a shower
it was absolutely beautiful to me

i was not chasing the rainbow anymore
but only viewing it for what it was
and then i was back to my daily life
and chores and enjoyments.

no more chasing rainbows for me
    and as for those people who still chase
        i will watch them and i will be cautious
            for i fear the rainbow chasers most of all.

I Chased Rainbows

I chased rainbows in my effort to attain
the one and only true way to God
and now I have ceased chasing rainbows

I chased rainbows for so long that I lost my way
and now I have quit chasing rainbows
and I have found my way home.

About the Author

Tony Prewit was born in Stamford, Texas in 1954 and then moved with his family at the age of eight to Silver City, New Mexico. He has earned both bachelor's and master's of arts degrees and has traveled extensively throughout the United States as a musician. Besides his interest in poetry, the author has written, directed, and performed in several plays and as a mime actor. In addition, he is an artist who delves in photography, charcoals, pastels, and watercolors. Art is his private therapy.

For over thirty-five years the author kept a jounal of poetry that chronicled his most secret, inner struggles with his belief in God. During that time he lived what seemed to be a fairly normal life—traveling, going to school, marrying, and owning a retail furniture company. This journal, however, does not chronicle his "normal" life, but his struggles with belief. He believes many people have these same kinds of inner challenges with life, and this journal brings to the forefront the reality of these challenges.

Since 1978 he has lived with his wife Pat, a classical pianist, in Silver City, New Mexico, the place he considers home for its culture, land, seasons, and people.